Frank E. Edwards

The '98 campaign of the 6th Massachusetts, U. S. V.

Frank E. Edwards

The '98 campaign of the 6th Massachusetts, U. S. V.

ISBN/EAN: 9783337810368

Printed in Europe, USA, Canada, Australia, Japan

Cover: Foto ©ninafisch / pixelio.de

More available books at **www.hansebooks.com**

THE '98 CAMPAIGN

OF THE

6th Massachusetts, U.S.V.

BY

LIEUT. FRANK E. EDWARDS

With 70 Illustrations from Original Photographs

BOSTON
LITTLE, BROWN, AND COMPANY
1899

Copyright, 1899,
By Little, Brown, and Company

All rights reserved

University Press
John Wilson and Son, Cambridge, U.S.A.

Introduction

THE Spanish-American War of 1898 was the justification of the Massachusetts Volunteer Militia. When Governor Wolcott sent to Washington to ascertain what would be required of the Commonwealth in case war was declared, he was informed by General Miles that the militia of the coast States would in all probability be used only for coast defence, and that the militia of the interior States would be used for any foreign expedition that might be determined upon.

This policy was almost instantly abandoned upon the outbreak of war, because it was found that the militia of the interior States, with some exceptions, were neither equipped nor drilled, and Massachusetts gladly did not only her own particular work, but the work originally cut out for others. The country asked Massachusetts to strip herself of her trained soldiers for the use of the Nation, and no more selfish policy was allowed to exist by the people of the State or the soldiers sprung from among them.

But one regiment mustered into the National service was used for coast defence, and of the four others summoned on the first call, three saw active and all saw foreign service. This, I believe, is a larger proportion than any other State actually sent to the front. It was not due to favoritism in Washington. It was due to the fact that the spirit of patriotic enthusiasm among the young men of Massachusetts had overcome popular ridicule, had swept beyond the dress tunic and bouquet-in-the-gun-barrel stage of military existence, and had produced a body of soldiers. Dress uniforms had been for years discarded for camp work, applied tactics had taken the place of parade, and *kriegspiel* and rifle practice had elbowed out "social events."

So-called "militia companies" from some States came to the front with less than ten per cent of their original members. There was more than one instance of a whole regiment's ignominiously turning tail when asked to face something besides the flutter of handkerchiefs and a brass band. From such experiences this Commonwealth was free. Massachusetts had been for years steadily weeding out the parade soldier from her ranks, and the result was not delay in filling her quota, but serious embarrassment in deciding who should not go. The six regiments and the naval brigade mustered from this State into the National service were not a mere uniformed mob of greenhorns, but every one of them a trained organization, their ranks increased to the proper size largely by the re-enlistment of former members. In more than one instance, men who had been discharged as officers re-enlisted as privates.

The troops of Massachusetts saw, proportionately, more of the war in the West Indies than the troops from any other State, simply because they reported for duty better armed, better equipped, better trained than the troops from any other State. The Commonwealth had steadily pressed home upon the militia the notion that the muster field was a workshop, not a picnic grove, and when the emergency came Massachusetts found that her grimy old fatigue uniforms covered men.

Among the four regiments of infantry selected on the first call was the Sixth. A general order had suggested to company commanders the advisability of sounding their companies and collecting the names of additional volunteers to fill the required quota. A meeting of officers was called at the State House at the same hour that the Colonel was called to confer with the Governor. Colonel Woodward walked from the

Governor's room straight into the meeting of his officers. Every officer was present or accounted for. The Governor's selection was declared, the roll was called, and a report from each company and the field music made. One hour after Governor Wolcott delegated the Colonel of the Sixth Infantry to raise a volunteer regiment, the Adjutant of the Sixth was in the office of Adjutant General Dalton with the report that the regiment was raised, that every officer, line, field, and staff, had volunteered, and that the Colonel requested the services of a medical examiner and a mustering officer.

This request was not granted. The infantry regiments were sent to camp according to the seniority of their colonels,—the Sixth being the the last of all. The bitter cold of those spring nights and the short supply of blankets were a foretaste of real campaigning, but were cheerfully endured. The spirit of Massachusetts was shown by men who broke down and wept like children when denied by the stern decree of the army surgeon the envied privilege of bearing arms for the flag.

The richest civilized nation asked its sons to fight with obsolete weapons against men whom the poorest civilized nation had equipped with ordnance of the latest pattern. Yet the only

Introduction ix

tears that fell came from those who were not allowed to carry the Springfield against the Mauser.

It is not surprising that even the most censorious of war correspondents should have, in his history of the war, set down of material like this when under fire

"The Sixth Massachusetts behaved well."

CURTIS GUILD, Jr.

The Army

"ON the 1st day of April, 1898, the strength of the army was 2,143 officers and 26,040 enlisted men, a total of 28,183. War with the kingdom of Spain was declared April 21, 1898.

"On May 31, 125,000 volunteers had been mustered into the service. In August, 1898, the regular army numbered 56,365, the volunteer army 207,244, — a total of 263,609.

"These figures of themselves indicate that an immense work was thrown upon the War Department. After thirty-three years of peace, during a great part of which the army did not exceed 26,000 men, it suddenly became necessary to arm, clothe, feed, and equip more than a quarter of a million.

"The sudden emergency which called our people to arms after an interval of half a century of peace with all foreign powers was met by the War Department with earnestness and energy. The situation found the country unprepared with any large stock of arms, ammunition, clothing, supplies, and equipments. That they were duly provided, and that the numerous demands on the industries of our people were met so promptly, will remain one of the marvels of history."

Preface

THE history of every regiment is dear to its members, while to those which have received the baptism of fire it becomes sacred.

The history of the 6th Massachusetts in the Spanish-American War is unique in that its campaign was almost a bloodless one, the absence of battles and the few months it was in the field rendering its experiences different in kind and degree from those regiments which were in the Civil War almost as many years, and even from its sister regiments in Cuba in '98. And while the following account is written with a full appreciation of the seemingly insurmountable difficulties overcome by the War Department in an incredibly short space of time, in addition to the necessary hardships of army life, and is not intended in any sense as a "lament," there is that to record of interest not only to the regiment itself but to its friends.

Deprived of the tonic of battles and a dangerous environment, the life of the regiment became one of existence in a land of plenty; but, owing to the distance and difficulty of communication with home, and the fact that no pay had been received for three months, the men were unable to help out the scant army rations with the simplest fare. Discouragement was only averted by the consciousness that Uncle Sam was ignorant of the life of his children, and would disapprove it, together with the comfort that came in the message sent by Governor Wolcott to the President "that the lives of her sons are precious in the eyes of the Commonwealth," and that when the health of her soldiers is at stake, Massachusetts feels that "no effort can be too great, and no expenditure too lavish." The men hoped as long as the war was over and the country did not need the lives which they had freely offered, that they might at least so live as to return home with sound bodies. The perspective of a year has softened the harsh lines of experience, and the regiment again in health views the long list of casualties of other regiments and feels thankful that the chapter "In Memoriam" contains no other names.

For this reason the story has been told rather as a narrative than by the sharp-cut events of the daily diary of a fighting campaign.

The trail has been rough in places, and at times the load so heavy as to make it desirable to drop unnecessary burdens. I have finished the course with the principal outfit, trusting to the kindly judgment of those with whom I have walked in the ranks for the sake of all concerned not to ask for the abandoned articles.

Acknowledgments are due to many for photographs and letters, also to the press for courtesies received. If any paragraphs appear without credit to the writer, it is unintentional.

Contents

Chapter		Page
I.	The Call for Service	1
II.	Reception in Baltimore	11
III.	Camp Alger	25
IV.	The "Yale"	45
V.	Guanica	74
VI.	Resignation of Officers at Ponce	90
VII.	Utuado	132
VIII.	The Hospitals	186
IX.	The "Bay State"	206
X.	Arecibo	224
XI.	Porto Rico	242
XII.	Homeward Bound	259
Roster		293
In Memoriam		333

List of Illustrations

	PAGE
Colonel Edmund Rice	*Frontispiece*
Troops Passing through Boston	5
Governor Wolcott Presenting the Commissions	8
Maryland and Massachusetts. Baltimore Welcomes the 6th Mass. Reg't.	11
6th Mass. at Mt. Royal Station, B. & O. Railroad, Baltimore	17
Maryland's Greeting to Massachusetts	21
Camp Alger	27
Shaving under Difficulties	41
Admiral Sampson and General Miles	46
"The Yale"	47
On Board the "Yale"	57
A Shower Bath	63
The Harbor of Guanica	70
Major Edward J. Gihon	83
Major General Nelson A. Miles	91
Spanish Block-House	95
Native Laundry	96
H. W. Gross	97
Five Minutes' Rest	101
After Cocoanuts	103
"Brace up, Boys, there's Old Glory!"	107
A Company Street	108
A Group of Natives	110
Colonel Charles Woodward	113
Headquarters	116
Major Charles K. Darling	117

List of Illustrations

	PAGE
Mr. Dwight L. Rogers, of the Y. M. C. A.	121
Map of Porto Rico	133
Road from Ponce to Harbor	135
Colonel Edmund Rice	137
A Native Express	139
"Dutch Yoke"	140
"A Porto Rican Picnic"	141
Natives Bathing at "Mud Hole"	150
Utuado	151
The Soldiers' Cemetery, Utuado	155
Frederic A. Washburn	157
Mrs. Colonel Rice	161
Heavy Marching Order Inspection	163
Utuado Market Scene	167
Going to the Concert	168
Sunday in Utuado	174
A Native Pack Train	176
Chaplain George D. Rice	179
Starting for Outpost Duty	182
Governor Wolcott	183
Native Water Carrier	185
Major George F. Dow	187
Hospital Laundry	194
Miss Muriel G. Galt	195
Dr. Crockett	198
Hospital Train for Arecibo	200
Convalescents on the Way to the "Bay State"	201
Hospital Stewards	203
Miss Sadie Parsons	221
Spanish Soldiers entertaining American Soldiers	225
Three of a Kind	227
Arecibo	229
Charity	234
Major George H. Priest	237
The Plaza in Utuado	245

List of Illustrations

xix

	PAGE
A Suburban Residence	250
San Juan, Porto Rico	261
The "Mississippi"	271
The Fitchburg Banquet Hall	279
Lieut. Col. Butler Ames	283
Statue of Columbus, San Juan	287
Major E. J. Gihon, 2d Lt. F. E. Edwards, 1st Lt. Louis D. Hunton	295
Captain Alexander Greig, 1st Lt. Thomas Livingston, 2d Lt. Fred D. Costello	301
Captain Warren E. Sweetser, 1st Lt. George R. Barnstead, 2d Lt. Henry A. Thayer	313
Captain Cyrus H. Cook	317
Captain W. J. Williams, 1st Lt. W. H. Jackson, 2d Lt. G. W. Braxton	323
2d Lieut. Arthur J. Draper	327
There's no Place like Home	331
Charles F. Parker, Myris H. Warren, George Tyler Cutting, George C. Wenden	337
Herbert C. Bellamy, John J. Delaney, William E. Walters	341
Willis H. Page, Ernest D. Marshall, John O. Cole, Leon E. Warren	345
Ralph Prescott Hosmer, George Edward Adams, Charles Abraham Hart, George Henry Sayles	349
Martin Welch, Charles Edward McGregor, John E. Riley, Patrick Kelly	353
Paul T. French, Asa B. Trask, Arthur L. Wilkinson, Charles E. Johnson	357

The '98 Campaign

OF

The 6th Massachusetts, U.S.V.

CHAPTER I

THE CALL FOR SERVICE

THAT long period of uncertainty and anxiety that preceded the declaration of war, when the national consciousness was struggling on the one hand to do its duty to a downtrodden people, and on the other to avert the horrors of war, was suddenly brought to an end by the tragedy of the blowing up of the "Maine." The investigation instituted by our government reported to Congress that she had been blown up by outside forces, but no formal charge was made against Spain for this act either then or later. Notwithstanding the tone of this report, the public at large was so strongly influenced by the calamity that, perhaps half unconsciously, it turned the balance of indecision to the side of action. That the unspoken opinion then formed has since become crystallized as fact is shown by one of our latest histories, which without reservation attributes the blowing up of the "Maine" to Spain.

The President, in his war message to Congress on the 25th of April, said: —

"I now recommend to your honorable body the adoption of a joint resolution declaring that a state of war exists between the United States of America and the Kingdom of Spain, and I urge speedy action thereon to the end that the definition of the international status of the United States as a belligerent power may be made known, and the assertion of all its rights and the maintenance of all its duties in the conduct of a public war may be assured.

[Signed] "WILLIAM McKINLEY."

This war bill was passed without delay, and immediately notice of it was sent to all the representatives of foreign nations.

Thus ended the period of suspense, and war, that most terrible of all words, which to the younger generation had become a tradition, was pronounced by the President as existing fact.

A new experience and problem was waiting for our nation. To be at war with a foreign race, on soil saturated with European traditions, with a foreign language to contend with, and in a climate and season sufficient in themselves to defeat an army, was not a cheerful or promising outlook.

Our army numbered but 25,000 men, and we must be prepared to resist not only attack at home over our great extent of coast-line east and west, but be able to place in the field for foreign service an army large enough to contend with both Spain and climates.

Our papers had for weeks emphasized the danger of tropical fevers, sunstrokes, lack of food, treacheries of natives, etc., so when the call for volunteers came, there was no man so ignorant but he was entirely familiar with the possibilities he had to face.

The war was to be primarily an aggressive one, and there was not that stimulus for men to enlist that comes when home and family are threatened by the enemy. On the other hand it was to be an enlistment that might mean Cuba or Manila, home service or Spain, sickness or death. On April the 23d the President issued the first call for 125,000 volunteers.

The proportion of men wanted for the war in '98 was to the number required in '61 from a given population only as one to fifty. This enabled the government to accept only men who were in a thoroughly good condition physically, and to place in the field regiments composed of practically picked men from a population not decimated or weakened by previous drafts.

Another and not the least element of strength which entered into the make-up of the army was the "moral" force of men having volunteered. There was no half-hearted obedience from drafted men, but the willing response of soldiers who offered freely and willingly their services, and lives if need be, for the good of their country, with an intelligent understanding of what they were doing. Doubtless there were cases of blustering and ignorant revengefulness shown, but this usually exhausted itself in the use of letter paper decorated with star-spangled banners, or in wearing suspenders embroidered with "Remember the Maine." These were the few. On the whole the regiments were enlisted in an atmosphere of cool judgment and good sense, as part of an army to stand by force, if necessary, for the righting of a national wrong. And the men individually, while not filled perhaps with the holy zeal of the Crusades of the Middle Ages, did have a strong sense of the honor of taking part in a crusade against the degradation and ignorance, resulting from a tyrannical government, and of supplanting it with the life and privileges belonging to an enlightened free people.

The make-up and motives actuating the regiments were essentially the same. Men from every walk in life filled the ranks, — the lawyer, the mechanic, the laboring-man, the college student, marching shoulder to shoulder. One of the stock questions asked one another was, "What induced

Troops Passing through Boston.

you to enlist?" The answers were as various as they were evasive, ranging all the way from the man who had dined "too well, but not wisely" and who had enlisted immediately after dinner, to the man whose avowed principal motive was patriotism. And if sympathy with the famous remark, "Our country! In her intercourse with foreign nations may she always be in the right; but our country, right or wrong!" can be called enlisting from patriotism, then the great majority of the men must have that credit, for it was for their country they enlisted.

"First in the field" was the motto of the "old 6th," and as worthy successors, the 6th Massachusetts, U. S. V., was the first regiment reporting to the Adjutant General of Massachusetts as being ready for service.

The call for volunteers was issued on the 23d of April, and the 6th of May found the regiment in camp at South Framingham, awaiting orders.

The twelve companies which composed the regiment were from the following towns and cities: Company A of Wakefield, Companies B and D of Fitchburg, Companies C and G of Lowell, Company E of South Framingham, Company F of Marlboro, Company H of Stoneham, Company I of Concord, Company K of Southbridge, Company L of Boston, and Company M of Milford.

On the 12th, Companies A, I, C, and F were mustered in by Lieutenant E. M. Weaver, U. S. A., the others on the day following.

Life at Camp Dewey was pleasant, as the nearness to home enabled the men to live comfortably, and the distance from the enemy eliminated night alarms. The days were passed in routine drill and the fulfilment of ordinary camp duties. The members of the 6th were fully conscious of the

GOVERNOR WOLCOTT PRESENTING THE COMMISSIONS.

position they occupied as the successors of the "old 6th," and that the eyes of the country would contrast the record of '98 with that of '61, and they asked that the mantle of the "old 6th" might fall on them. On the 18th, Governor Wolcott visited the camp, reviewed the troops, and presented the newly appointed officers with their commissions.

FIELD AND STAFF OFFICERS.

Charles F. Woodward, Colonel; George H. Chaffin, Lieutenant Colonel; George H. Taylor, Major; Charles K. Darling, Major; George H. Priest, Major; Curtis Guild, Jr., Adjutant; William Dusseault, Chaplain; Stanwood G. Sweetser, 1st Lieutenant and Quartermaster; Oris H. Marion, Major and Surgeon; George F. Dow, 1st Lieutenant and Assistant Surgeon; Frederick A. Washburn, Jr., 1st Lieutenant and Assistant Surgeon.

Later Adjutant Guild received an appointment on General Lee's staff, resigning his commission in the 6th, being succeeded by Lieutenant Butler Ames of Battery A. Two days later orders were received at 11 A. M. to move at once to Camp Alger. At 1 P. M. tents were struck, the ground policed, and at six o'clock the regiment was on the train at South Framingham *en route* for the South, having been reviewed by Governor Wolcott and his staff as it passed Fort Dalton. The regiment moved in three sections, a battalion making a section, with the field and staff officers and band in the first. Worcester, Springfield, and Pittsfield, each vied with one another in the hearty welcome they gave the troops as they passed through to New York by way of Albany.

In '61, when the 6th was making this same journey, word was received at Philadelphia of the reception it might expect in Baltimore. Likewise in '98, when Philadelphia was reached, a message was received from the Mayor of Baltimore, stating what treatment *this regiment* might expect at the hands of its citizens.

"Colonel C. F. Woodward, 6th Massachusetts Volunteers, *en route:* Have arranged reception and lunch. Short parade from Mt. Royal Station to Camden Station. Wire hour of your arrival.

"Mayor U. T. MALSTER."

Colonel Woodward also received a telegram from the War Department granting him permission to stop over at Baltimore and march across the city.

CHAPTER II

RECEPTION IN BALTIMORE

"Next come the Massachusetts men,
  Gathered from city, glade, and glen.
No hate for South, but love for all
They answered to their country's call.
The path to them seemed broad and bright,
They sought no foeman and no fight,
As on they marched, their flag before
New England's braves, through Baltimore."
            (*Dedicated to the 6th by J. W. Forney in '61.*)

SINCE leaving Boston, the regiment had met with an uninterrupted series of ovations at the stations it passed, being greeted with cheers and favors of a more substantial character wherever a stop was made. The patriotism of the country was at fever heat, and a uniformed regiment was the signal for showing it. Not until Baltimore was reached, however, did the regiment realize the  strength of feeling in that section of the country, or the full meaning of Southern patriotism. The memory of that famous march of the 6th Massachusetts through Baltimore in '61 was revived, and the eyes of the country were turned on that city to see what the sequel would be. Some even remembered the days when the following account appeared in every paper.

Colonel Jones' Official Report to Major W. H. Clemence.

WASHINGTON, D. C., Apr. 22, 1861.

After leaving Philadelphia I received intimation that our journey through Baltimore would be resisted. I caused ammunition to be distributed and arms loaded; and went personally through the cars and issued the following order:

"The regiment will march through Baltimore in columns of sections, arms at will. You will undoubtedly be insulted, abused and perhaps assaulted, to which you must pay no attention whatever; but march with your faces square to the front and pay no attention to the mob even if they throw stones, bricks, and other missiles: but if you are fired upon, and any one of you is hit, your officers will order you to fire. Do not fire into any promiscuous crowds, but select any man whom you see aiming at you, and be sure you drop him."

Reaching Baltimore, horses were attached the instant the locomotive was detached, and the cars were driven at a rapid pace across the city. After the cars containing seven companies had reached Washington depot the track behind them was barricaded, and the cars containing the band and the following companies — C, D, T, L — were vacated, and they proceeded to march in accordance with orders and had proceeded but a short distance before they were furiously attacked by a shower of missiles which came faster as they proceeded. They increased their step to double quick, which seemed to infuriate the mob, as it evidently impressed them with the idea that the soldiers did not dare fire, or had no ammunition. Pistol shots were fired from the ranks and one soldier fell dead.

The order "Fire" was given and it was executed, in consequence of which several of the mob fell and the soldiers advanced quickly. The Mayor of Baltimore placed himself at the head of the column beside Captain Follonsbee, and proceeded with them a short distance, assuring them that he would protect them, and begging him not to let the men fire; but the mayor's patience was soon exhausted, and he seized a musket from the hands of one of the men, and killed a man therewith; and a policeman who was in advance of the column also shot a man with a revolver. They at last reached the cars, and they started immediately for Washington. On going through the train I found there were about one hundred and thirty missing including the band and field music. Our baggage was seized and we have not as yet been able to recover any of it. I have found it very difficult to get reliable information in regard to the killed and wounded.

As the men went into the cars I caused the blinds to be closed, and took every precaution to prevent any shadow of offence to the people of Baltimore; but still the stones flew thick and fast into the train, and it was with the utmost difficulty that I could prevent the troops from leaving the cars and revenging the death of their comrades.

EDWARD F. JONES,
Colonel Sixth Regiment M. V. M. in service of U. S.

"When this news of the attack of the Sixth was received in Boston, the most intense excitement followed. Men gathered in groups about the streets, while crowds surrounded the bulletin boards of the newspapers to learn the particulars. If anything was needed to arouse the patriotism of the North, it had now occurred. Public meetings were held in various parts of the city; merchants, lawyers, physicians, and members of other professions met, and offers of service and money were offered for the use of the State by the Boston banks and banks of other cities for the State's immediate use, trusting to the honor of the legislature to reimburse them when it set. Numerous offers of money were made to the Governor by private individuals as aid for soldiers' families. Nor were women lagging behind the men in enthusiasm. Rich and poor, high and low, all offered their services for the preparation of bandages and lint, the making of garments, attendance in hospitals, or any other service compatible with their sex."

These old letters are inserted not in any degree to resurrect the skeleton of the "late unpleasantness" between North and South, but that the reception tendered the 6th in Baltimore in '98 may receive additional lustre from having the background of the history of '61.

When the train bearing the divisions of the 6th Massachusetts arrived in Baltimore, the crowd had spread over every inch of available ground, around up the slopes facing the station, giving the effect of a great amphitheatre, which

Reception in Baltimore

was brightened by the colors of summer gowns and bonnets and hundreds of bouquets of flowers. Under a blue sky floated innumerable flags in every direction, while the Fifth Regimental Corps Band, early on the ground, entertained the crowd with patriotic airs. "Dixie," "Yankee Doodle," "Maryland, my Maryland," and "The Star Spangled Banner," were all played and received equal applause, even if in the hearts of a few "Dixie" was responsible for a touch of sadness. Col. Frank Supplee was chairman of the arrangement committee, prominent among whom was Arthur George Brown, Esq., a son of George William Brown, who was Mayor of Baltimore in 1861, and who bravely marched at the head of the "6th" regiment when it was threatened by the mob. Amongst the citizens' committee also were a number of the Confederate Veterans' Association, who laughingly confessed to having thrown rocks in '61, but they were throwing flowers in '98.

When the regiment landed from the train it was to find itself in a station gay with national colors in every shape and form with streamers bearing the words, "A hearty welcome to the 6th Regiment." Another had the words, "Maryland and Massachusetts. The 5th is in the field, the 6th is coming." While a third bore the inscription of

Webster's immortal words, "Liberty and union, now and forever, one and inseparable."

When the regiment appeared, the enthusiasm of the people in and about the station was without limit. Women waved their handkerchiefs and men hugged each other and danced. The sound of the hoarse cheering outside, mingled with the strains of the band, floated into the station and gave the tired soldiers their first taste of true Maryland hospitality. It was known that a colored company was in the regiment, and there was an interrogation as to what its reception would be. But the wave of hospitable welcome with which the men were met broke over all barriers of race and color. All shared alike in the reception they received, and no one knew or cared whether a man was black or white, so long as he had 6 on his hat. The men were stupefied. One young soldier remarked: "You people make us ashamed of ourselves. We haven't done anything great. If we get half a chance, we will try to deserve something like this when we come back, but your reception is so warm that we feel as if we are sailing under false colors." Souvenirs of welcome were given to each man, of which the "cut" is a fac-simile. The battalion was formed upon the platform and the order to march was given, when they stepped out to the tune of "On the

6TH MASS. AT MT. ROYAL STATION, B. & O. RAILROAD, BALTIMORE.

Banks of the Wabash" and marched into the main plaza, where another storm of cheers, hand-clapping, waving of flags, and other demonstrations of enthusiasm were shown. Flowers, cigarettes, and cigars were showered upon the men without limit.

As the troopers marched out of the train-shed a graceful act was performed through the efforts of several members of the reception committee. Two small boys, Masters David Wilson Miller Glass and Ferdinand C. Latrobe, Jr., scattered over a bushel of roses and other flowers in their path amidst much cheering. It was a happy thought aptly carried to consummation, and the smiling faces of the soldiers showed that they appreciated the courtesy.

Mayor Malster was introduced to the members of the regiment by the marshal of the day — Colonel Supplee — and that official immediately began his address from the portico. He said : —

"Soldiers of the Sixth Massachusetts Regiment of Infantry, I join with the citizens of Baltimore to-day in the deferred opportunity of thirty-seven years of congratulating you and offering you the hospitality and protection of our beloved city. Soldiers of Massachusetts, the latch-string does not alone hang out of the doors of the citizens of Baltimore, but the door is open, and we ask you to come in. You need have no fear to-day. Look around you and you will see that there are none that would do anything that could wound even the most sensitive feeling. You have inherited the legacy left by the 'old 6th,' and we are sure you will prove yourselves worthy of that proud name. In history their names are written in the blood of patriots. You are now going to the front in the cause of humanity and right, but you are going against a foe that is not worthy of your steel. When you return, however, we hope that each individual will have made for himself a place in history, and I am sure that you will do so as the loyal sons of loyal fathers."

The Mayor then presented, in the following words, the magnificent floral tribute which had been secured for the command to Colonel Woodward, of the 6th regiment: —

"Colonel, I wish to present your command, in behalf of the citizens of Baltimore, with this small token of their good-will. I trust that you will not measure their feelings by the size of the gift, nor yet by its life, but I sincerely hope that its fragrance will cement forever the friendship of Maryland and Massachusetts."

Colonel Woodward accepted the gift on the part of the regiment in a few words.

"I have," he said, "no words with which I can adequately express my feeling in this matter, and appreciation for the honors which you are conferring upon us. The present war, if it has done nothing else, has had one grand and glorious effect: it has cemented the country as solid as a rock. To-day, from Maryland to Massachusetts, from the Lakes to the Gulf, from the

Reception in Baltimore

Atlantic to the Pacific, we are as one. I thank you again, good people of Baltimore, and God be with you now and forevermore."

The crowning event of the day, if it be possible to speak of one event over another as claiming that distinction, was this presentation to the regiment of a magnificent floral piece from the citizens of Baltimore. It was an immense bank of red and white roses artistically arranged on a litter and carried in the procession by two colored porters from the Mt. Royal station. The flowers were held in place by long streamers of blue and white ribbon, bearing the following inscription:

> "Maryland honors Massachusetts.
> Baltimore welcomes 6th Mass.
> God preserve you and bring you safely home."

When leaving, every man, as he boarded the train, was handed a box of luncheon, in each of which was a card bearing the following words of welcome:

Maryland's Greeting to Massachusetts.

Baltimore and Boston Clasp Hands.

...6th Massachusetts Volunteers,...

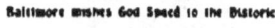

Do We Love You?—Dewey.   Baltimore, May 21, 1898.

The stimulus of adversity being removed from the regiment, they followed in the wake of all such experiences. Outposts were forgotten in sight of the decorated interiors, and guards were asking the password from the sex who are supposed to figure in war only in the hospitals. The entire regiment fell to eating and drinking, and became an easy subject for the enemy.

The good resolutions of emulating the example of the " old 6th " were entirely forgotten, and, as great warriors have been known to do before, so the 6th in the light of the eyes of Baltimore went to pieces. Yes, almost literally; for when they boarded the train nothing but their cartridge belts kept their coats on, for all their buttons had been left in Baltimore. But the Capitol was not waiting to be saved, and there was no prospect of sleeping in " Speakers' " chairs, or of lunching off the Honorables' desks as the " old 6th " had done.

Much that was written regarding the march through Baltimore in '61, though conceived in a different spirit, is applicable to the changed condition existing to-day. Thus may the following lines be appropriated: —

" Whatever rank among the conflicts of the late war the march of the ever famous 6th through Baltimore may, as a military movement, ultimately assume, it can never fail to confer proud distinction upon its heroes from its peculiarity of *time, place, and incidents*."

Reception in Baltimore

This reception was without question the most dramatic event of the war on American soil. For it was not a mere reception and patriotic demonstration. It was the new national spirit rising Phœnix-like from the ashes of '61. It was not Baltimore and Massachusetts alone joining hands, it was the meeting of the conservative representatives of a New South and a New North under circumstances of the deepest import in a national crisis.

Senator Henry Cabot Lodge, who had gone over from Washington to meet the regiment, said:—

"Baltimore has made history. She has let fall a rosebud of affection which will touch the heart of the entire nation. No city but Baltimore could have performed such an act. She has lifted up her name to the very pinnacle of renown. Upon that over-topping monument of splendid fraternal patriotism the entire world may gaze and see there for themselves the character and splendor of our people."

Adapted from Verses of '61.

"The sons of Massachusetts they marched unto the war,
And on that day upon the way they stopped at Baltimore,
And trustingly expected the customary cheers
Which every loyal city gave the Yankee volunteers.

"So *generous* grew the multitude they rushed at them amain
And a great storm of *flowers* came pouring down like rain,
And a thundering clamor such as mortal seldom hears.
They tried to cross the city, did the Yankee volunteers.

"Those very numerous *luncheons* laid many a soldier low,
Still the kindly hearts forbore to give the fatal blow
Till all the people shouted, 'They're nearly dead from cheers,
We'll hurry up and finish those Yankee volunteers.'"

Then unto each brave soldier a little box was given
That showed a long blue card where the lid was riven:
"Do we love you? Dewey." — The soldiers said that great
Like all the rest in Baltimore in 1898.

"*To the Mayor of Baltimore :* —

"The Commonwealth of Massachusetts is profoundly touched by the brotherly and enthusiastic welcome extended by the mayor and citizens of Baltimore to the Sixth Massachusetts Regiment, United States Volunteers. In the name of the Commonwealth I beg you to accept her grateful thanks.
"ROGER WOLCOTT."

CHAPTER III

CAMP ALGER

WASHINGTON not being reached until late in the evening, there was no formal parade, the regiment crossing directly to the station where the Dun Loring train was waiting, and boarded it as tired as a lot of schoolboys after a holiday. A block in the road delaying the train the troops remained on board until the following morning, when they marched directly to the camp, and were assigned the location just vacated by the District of Columbia troops.

The environment of the camp was far from being in a proper condition for troops, and a polluted stream bordering the grounds added to the danger of the situation. Drinking water had to be carried a long distance from wells and springs until artesian wells were sunk near the camp, after which a bountiful supply of good water was obtained.

The regiment had wall tents, good food, and was as comfortable as could be expected in the heat and dust of Virginia in June. Passes were issued for the men to go to Washington, giving all who desired it a chance to visit the Capitol.

On the 22d of May, Lieut. Butler Ames received the appointment of adjutant of the regiment as successor to Curtis Guild, Jr., who had resigned his commission, and was immediately appointed by Major General Graham as corps engineer officer, with instructions to devote all the time he could spare from his regimental duties to securing a proper supply of water. Artesian wells were driven in different parts of the camp, the first one being near the camp of the 6th, and this one gave a plentiful supply of good water for the 6th Massachusetts and the 8th Ohio regiments, which were camped on adjoining sites.

May the 22d was a gala day, as President McKinley, Secretary Alger, General Miles, and a number of members of the Cabinet visited the camp and reviewed the troops, expressing themselves as greatly pleased with the appearance of the brigade, of which the 8th Ohio, the "President's own," enrolled two of the President's nephews as privates.

On May 24 the 6th was brigaded with the 6th Illinois and the 8th Ohio; and, pending the arrival of a brigade commander, Col. D. Jack Foster of the 6th Illinois, being the senior colonel, was placed in command.

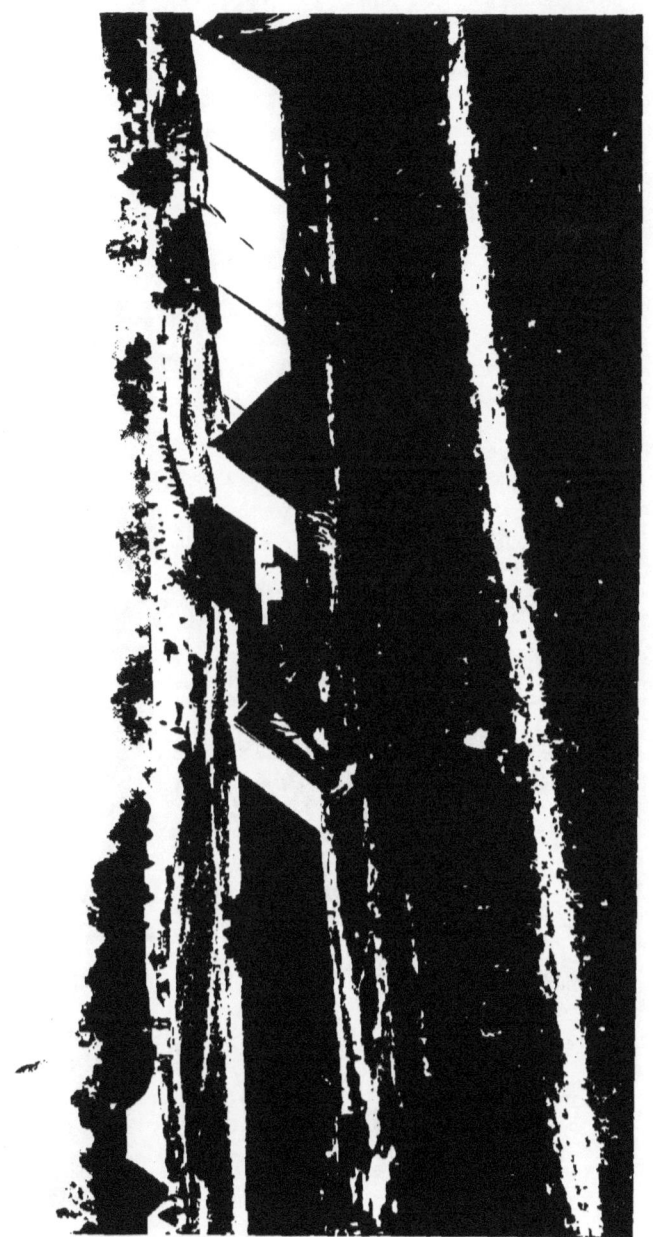

Camp Alger.

The next day a flag, presented by Congressman Sprague, who had previously shown his friendship for the regiment by the gift of several hundred gallons of spring water, was raised on a 70-foot pole which had been erected for the purpose near the colonel's headquarters. As Congressman Sprague was unable to be present, Congressman McCall made the presentation speech, and Colonel Woodward raised the flag to the accompaniment of three rousing cheers from the men.

FROM "COOLIDGE."

WASHINGTON, May 25.

There was a flag-raising in the camp of the 6th to-day, and it was the most impressive incident thus far in the life of Camp Alger. It was not an ordinary flag-raising. The banner which was flung out in the May sun this afternoon was cheered and saluted by a thousand Massachusetts boys whose presence there was a pledge of their willingness to die in its defence. And it may be in the chances of war that every one of those who reverently bared their heads as the Stars and Stripes shot up the staff will soon be called on to put his pledge to the test. The flag was the gift of Congressman Sprague. It was brought to camp this morning by Mr. Baker, the Congressman's secretary, and presented by him to Colonel Woodward. It is much larger and handsomer than any of the other flags in camp, and as it flies conspicuously from the top of the knoll on which the regiment have raised their tents it is one of the most beautiful sights for miles around.

To Company F, from Marlboro, was assigned the honor of raising the flag, and they cut a pole nearly seventy feet high in the neighboring woods and placed it on the very summit of the knoll. When the time came for the raising, all the men in the regiment gathered around the pole in a great circle. Captain Jackson of the Marlboro Company let loose the flag while the fifes and drums played the "Star Spangled Banner." The men stood with uncovered heads, and Major Marion, the regimental surgeon, who had the ceremonies in charge, presented Representative McCall, who had been asked by Congressman Sprague to say a few words appropriate to the occasion.

Mr. McCall's speech was a model of simple and affecting eloquence, and more than once he was interrupted by cheers.

Mr. McCall spoke of Mr. Sprague's act of generosity and patriotism, and said that he himself could better learn patriotism than teach it in the presence of the brave men of the 6th Regiment. "You have shown your devotion," he said, " to the flag we have just raised by offering to face the perils of battle, and the possibly more deadly perils of climate, in the service of your country. You come from a State that is justly proud of her institutions, her citizenship, and her glorious history, but her people take a yet loftier pride in our common country, and above the white flag of Massachusetts they put the Stars and Stripes. She has loyally responded to the call of the President by promptly filling her quota with her best-disciplined and best-equipped troops, with such men as fill your ranks and make you the worthy successor of that regiment whose historic name you bear. We cannot foretell what may be the destiny of the flag which you proudly raise to-day, but of this we feel sure, that it will never come down in dishonor. In the keeping of your strong arms and brave hearts its lustre will remain undimmed. We fervently hope that you may return with ranks unbroken; but whatever may befall, we know that your record will form a bright page in the history of your State and in the history of your country."

Colonel Woodward responded, the Fife and Drum Corps played "America," and the men sang it with a will. Then there were cheers for Mr. Sprague, for Mr. McCall, for the colonel, for all the officers of the regiment, and for everybody imaginable, including the regiment's mascot; and the men dispersed to the routine duties of the camp.

On June 1, the 9th Massachusetts regiment arrived at Camp Alger, and went into camp about two miles from the 6th.

The 2d brigade of the 1st division, of which the 6th was a part, had been placed under command of Brigadier General George A. Garretson of Ohio, a personal friend of both President McKinley and Secretary Alger, and it was thought that this brigade, being the best equipped and best drilled in camp, would be the first to be sent to the front.

On June 7 the recruiting detail, consisting of Majors Taylor and Darling, Captain Cook, and one private or non-commissioned officer from each company, left for Boston to recruit the regiment to full war strength of 1327 men, 32 men being needed in each company. A few days later Paymaster Bailey of Massachusetts arrived in camp and paid the men the money given them by the State, and on June 17 the men received their first pay from the United States government.

The 17th of June was a holiday at camp, and was properly observed as it should be by Massachusetts men. A baseball game between teams from the 6th and 9th regiments was played in the morning, and a long programme of athletic sports was carried out in the afternoon. All camp duty except guard mount was omitted, and the men had nothing to do except to enjoy themselves all day. In the evening there was a display of fireworks in the camp of the 9th, refreshments were served, and the band of one of the Michigan regiments played in front of Colonel Bogan's headquarters until "taps."

Dr. Marion resigned his commission July 25, together with Lieut. Charles E. Walton of Co. A. Surgeon Dow succeeded to the rank of Major in place of Dr. Marion, while Surgeon Washburn took Dr. Dow's place, making a vacancy in the medical staff which was immediately filled by the appointment of Dr. Herman Gross of Brookline.

The certainty of the regiment's going into service brought into the ranks a number of men who were waiting until they were sure it was not going to summer in the States before enlisting. Among the recruits enlisted by the officers who returned to the North was a large percentage of college men, of which Company A claimed ten from Harvard alone. Each company was recruited to its full allowance of one hundred and six men, all in fine condition, restless in the delay of the order to move. The seeming slowness in filling up the ranks was due to the severe tests applied to recruits, the physical examinations being of the most searching character.

The arrival of every new squad of recruits was heralded at the entrance of camp by the cry of "Rookies!" And as the newly enlisted man with his breast swelling with patriotism and his heart beating rapidly passed in review down the company street subject to an inspection more searching than any official one, he was greeted with encouraging cries of "You'll be sorry." "I had a good home and I left it," etc. After reporting at headquarters each recruit was assigned to quarters in tent No. ——, where whatever guying he might have to meet, he was sure of finding good fellows who gladly shared food, bedding, etc., and who became his tutors during his novitiate until he had learned the ropes and was quite ready to extend a similar welcome to the next "rookie."

It was here that the story was told of the western private whose martial education had been in town and not at the front, when approached one night by General Garretson, visiting the guard, surprised him by the challenge of "Here comes de main Guy; turn out de push."

The camp at this time numbered over 10,000 men, and was indeed a white city, with its streets reaching over the knolls into the pine woods, where half screened by the trees the colors marked the regimental headquarters.

The neighing of horses, the rattle of empty wagons, tramp of the troops, while above all sounded the ceaseless roll of drums or practice of bands, with all the necessary accompaniments of a great camp, made a life of activity comparable to nothing outside the army. Entire streets, bordered with restaurants, jewellers, photographers, seemed to spring up in a night, while a theatre and the Y. M. C. A. and Salvation Army tents added to the cosmopolitan aspect of the place.

There was talk of marching the brigade to the transports, across the State, and a probability of there being plenty of work to do in the near future; so a preliminary march was made to the Potomac, the men going in heavy marching order and spending the night in their dog tents.

The move was made in every detail as though in the enemy's country, with an advance guard, wagon train heavily guarded, etc. The men slept on their arms ready to repulse the attack of any enemy that materialized, but were disappointed in being able to sleep undisturbed.

The 6th started to return to Camp Alger about 11 o'clock on the 28th, having left the temporary camp at Ball's Hill on the Potomac at 6.10 in the morning, about an hour in advance of the two other regiments in the brigade. The plan was to have the 6th Massachusetts take up a position on the road and try to prevent the 8th Ohio and 6th Illinois from reaching Camp Alger.

The 6th took its stand about four miles from camp and awaited the coming of the others. Blank cartridges had been provided, and orders were issued that all firing should cease when the regiments were within 50 feet of each other. The 8th Ohio boys became so excited, however, that they charged up to within three feet of the 6th Massachusetts, and during the scrimmage one of the Bay State boys, Private Harvey Reed, of Company B, received a painful wound from the wad of a blank cartridge. A member of the 8th Ohio fired into his face, blowing away part of his ear and filling his cheek and eyes full of powder.

It was thought at first that Reed would lose his eyesight, but fortunately this was not the case, although he was not able to return to duty for some time.

Major Weybrecht of the 8th Ohio, who commanded the attacking forces, received a painful powder burn on the back of the neck, and one of the 8th Ohio boys had his hand badly cut by a sword.

The 3d battalion of the 6th Massachusetts did outpost duty the night before at Ball's Hill, and was so watchful that the cavalry, who were hovering around the limits of the camp, could find no opening to make an attack.

When the 6th Massachusetts was marching toward camp, before the sham battle took place, it met another brigade starting out for a route march. The 3d Missouri had the rear guard in this brigade, and refused to let the 6th boys through its lines.

One company of Missourians drew up in company front across the road, and their captain halted Company H of the 6th, which was acting as advance guard. Captain Sweetser expostulated in vain. The Missouri captain said he had orders to let no one through the lines, and he intended to obey them. Colonel Woodward and Adjutant Ames rode up and tried to induce the captain to withdraw his men, but all to no purpose.

Some of the Missourians seized the colonel's and adjutant's horses by the head, and for a few moments it looked as if there would be serious trouble. Finally Colonel Woodward, seeing that neither argument nor persuasion would prevail, gave the order to the 6th Massachusetts boys to force their way through. The men fixed bayonets and started in column of fours, and the Missouri troops were forced to give way.

While Company F was on outpost duty, their headquarters were at the plantation occupied by General Sheridan during the civil war.

June 30, taps had been blown and only an occasional murmur of voices told of a few men who were still lying awake when suddenly the report of rifles and the assembly call was heard, followed by the first sergeant calling for companies to fall in as they were. The roll was called, and every man who did not respond was marked and the list sent to headquarters. We were then ordered to turn in and go to sleep. The cause was afterwards learned. A crowd of soldiers were loose in Washington, and the War Department had ordered a roll-call at Camp Alger to learn the names of the men who were out.

The tentage furnished by the State of Massachusetts to the regiment on muster in, upon inspection at Camp Alger, was condemned and by order was left on the ground for use of future occupants. New tentage was supplied at Dun Loring which was taken with the regiment's baggage to

Porto Rico, and eventually unloaded at Ponce, where by the order of General Henry it was stored and left.

Most of the companies' and a part of the regiment's boxes were never found, although a thorough search was made in the holds of all accessible transports.

The half-shelter tents, commonly known as dog or pup tents, which were given the men here, were used as the outside cover for the rolls, and on camping two of them were buttoned together to form a tent, to enter which it was necessary to get down on all fours and crawl in. That such a little shelter should ever come to be considered with any degree of affection or look attractive seemed at first sight impossible, but later the men learned after a long day's march or during a storm, that even a shelter tent had a degree of privacy and protection that savored of their own rooms at home.

Singing, as in all camps, was a favorite pastime with the men, and the regiment was fortunate in having an unusual number of good voices. Each company had its glee club, and after supper, as night fell, you were sure to hear from every street the familiar choruses by the men, varied by occasional solos by the best singers. " Break the News to Mother," " Say Au Revoir," " Nearer, my God, to

Thee," "Marching through Georgia," "The Old Oaken Bucket," etc., were favorites of an endless repertoire. The singing on shipboard later when the men were thrown more closely together was particularly good.

After numerous false rumors had raised the expectations of the men as to leaving, on July 5th the order came to strike tents, and the evening of that day found the men on board the train *en route* for Charleston, in cars that no emigrant company would dare place in service to-day. Dirty as they were on leaving camp, at the end of the run to Charleston 24 hours later, during which time the men, being provided with travelling rations, had not been allowed to leave their assigned cars, they were in a condition that I would not wish to picture to my readers, even if their imaginations were capable of reproducing it.

We reached Charleston at eight o'clock in the evening, but were kept in the cars until the following afternoon, alongside a Western regiment whose train, composed entirely of sleeping cars, pulled in next to ours, having casks of ice water on every platform. During the night a number of men got out of the car windows and went into the town for food and drink.

"And if sometimes our conduck isn't all your fancy paints,
Why, single men in barricks don't grow into plaster saints."

The following afternoon we were quartered in a hot, foul-smelling warehouse, where the only water, we were told, was not fit to drink, yet no other was provided. All who could, got passes to go into the city for supper, and to make last purchases for personal use.

The half dozen men who were fortunate enough to get to the hotel for a square meal were informed after dinner that privates about the hotel were *de trop* in the presence of the officials who were there. As going on the street meant being run in, the only alternative was resorted to of returning to the warehouse.

The men of the 6th are not angels but they are average men, and the severe attack made by some of the newspapers on the regiment was unjustifiable both in its description of the existing condition of affairs in the city, and in not stating the fact that there were six thousand troops there at the time. The following letter published in the "Globe" under date of July 8, describes the condition of affairs as seen by an outsider: —

CHARLESTON. S. C., July 7.

To-night there are nearly six thousand troops sleeping on the docks in this city under sheds and in warehouses. The former get all the air there is going, that is very little, while the latter are suffering considerably from the heat.

All day long the troops have had to stand on the

wharf, suffering from the heat and the want of a cool drink, while the 6th Massachusetts has been cooped up all day in the trains that brought the men here.

The command arrived here last night at 8.30, and it was just 10.15 to-night when the last company was allowed to leave the train and put foot on terra firma, making a total of $25\frac{3}{4}$ hours the boys had to remain in old stuffy cars that are relics of the past.

The trains full of soldiers stood in almost tropical heat for $25\frac{3}{4}$ hours, and then the men were put up in

SHAVING UNDER DIFFICULTIES.

a place not fit for a Christian to sleep in, while there are many vacant lots where the men might have pitched their tents and been comfortable all day and got in two good nights' rest. One officer said to-night. "God help us, if this is the kind of treatment we may expect when we reach Cuba."

At midnight the boys of the 6th were sleeping soundly, with the exception of the guard.

Colonel Woodward and staff to-day established headquarters at the Charleston hotel, and several of the line officers intended to spend the night there, while others went across the street to the St. Charles hotel. At ten o'clock General Garretson ordered that every line officer in his brigade should sleep with the men, and Adjutant Ames started off in a hack to notify the officers of the 6th, and all had to give up their beds and join their commands. Major Taylor of the 6th Massachusetts arrived this evening and reported for duty to Colonel Woodward. He received a cordial welcome from his brother officers.

To-day Captain Williams of Company L was considerably worse, and Surgeons Dow and Washburn advised the captain to go to the hospital. A hack was procured and this evening before midnight the captain was improved, and the surgeons in charge hope to have him in condition to go with the regiment to-morrow.

J. HARRY HARTLEY.

"Many stories of how the swiftest gang of soldiers spent the night were heard yesterday. In one place on Market St. there is a little slot machine which has made a harvest for its owner. Hundreds of nickels have been dropped in and few have come out. At 3 A. M. yesterday half a dozen soldiers met in the place to have some fun. One of them started off by dropping nickels in the slot. He slipped in five and the pocket refused to open. He was just about ready to drop in the sixth when a big, tall fellow said, 'T' 'ell wid de slot,' and grabbed it in his arms and disappeared. The other soldiers followed, while the proprietor of the place yelled and screamed for the police to catch the robbers. The soldiers, however, got safely away. Result, division of $2.00.

"Another misdemeanor: A young woman was walking through the market yesterday reading a paper. She was not paying much attention to what was going on about her until she happened to glance up and found a soldier walking quietly beside her. He asked her about the news. The young woman gave the soldier a withering look, when he dropped back a little and said, 'Oh, I don't know,' and walked away.

"The soldiers had money to burn and they left stacks of ashes. They had just been paid off before starting South, and rolls of healthy green bills were flaunted from the car windows in the faces of the people in the street. The men felt as if they were doing their last bit of blowing, and as one of them said, 'What the H — do we want with stuff in Cuba? We can steal it there.' This was the way they looked at the situation, and so when they struck the streets and stores the first thing to be done was to shake the stuff for something to make the owners thereof feel good."

When the regiment was ready to leave the following morning, the doctors pronounced Captain Williams too ill to be moved, so Company L left with Lieutenant Jackson in command, Captain Williams remaining in the hospital in Charleston until September, when he returned to Boston.

On Friday, what threatened to cause a break in the regiment by the leaving of some men on the wharf, after two detachments had already been sent to the "Yale," leaving but one company to be transported, was averted only by the prompt action of Adjutant Butler Ames, who remained with one company and who after the departure of the steamer was informed that it could not possibly make another trip that night. As he knew the "Yale" was to sail that night, immediately after the arrival of General Miles, the adjutant, with his characteristic promptness, seeing a tug tied up on the wharf near by, rushed over and chartered it, and placing Company F of Marlboro on board, amid the cheers of thousands of citizens and soldiers steamed out of the harbor to the "Yale," where he was given a welcome reception.

CHAPTER IV

THE "YALE"

ON the morning of July 8 we were taken on board ferryboats seven miles down the Charleston harbor, past Fort Sumter to where the "Yale," formerly the "City of Paris," lay waiting for us. We boarded her in a violent thunderstorm, and the entire regiment, excepting officers, together with one company of the 6th Illinois, were quartered on deck under the protection of "The Eli" and the "Handsome Dan," which bristled over her forward decks, being the guns presented to her by the students of Yale.

At midnight General Miles and his staff arrived from Washington, and immediately after the "Yale" started for Cuba. The run down was uneventful, all minds being filled with one idea, and a contemplation of the expected conflict as the consummation of the days of preparation. We passed San Salvador, the first landing-place of Columbus, but it excited little interest, as the men felt about Columbus as Tom Sawyer did about Adam, i.e., that he had been dead some time, and they wanted to see a *live* Spaniard.

On the afternoon of the 10th a steamer was sighted going North. The "Yale" signalled, asking for news, and received the reply: "Continuous heavy fighting in front of Santiago for two days."

ADMIRAL SAMPSON AND GENERAL MILES.

Early the next morning Cape Maysi was sighted, and during the forenoon the "Yale" passed Guantanamo, where the marines were encamped, and Baiquiri, where the first landing of troops took place. But when we descried in the distance the puffs of smoke rising from the battleships lying

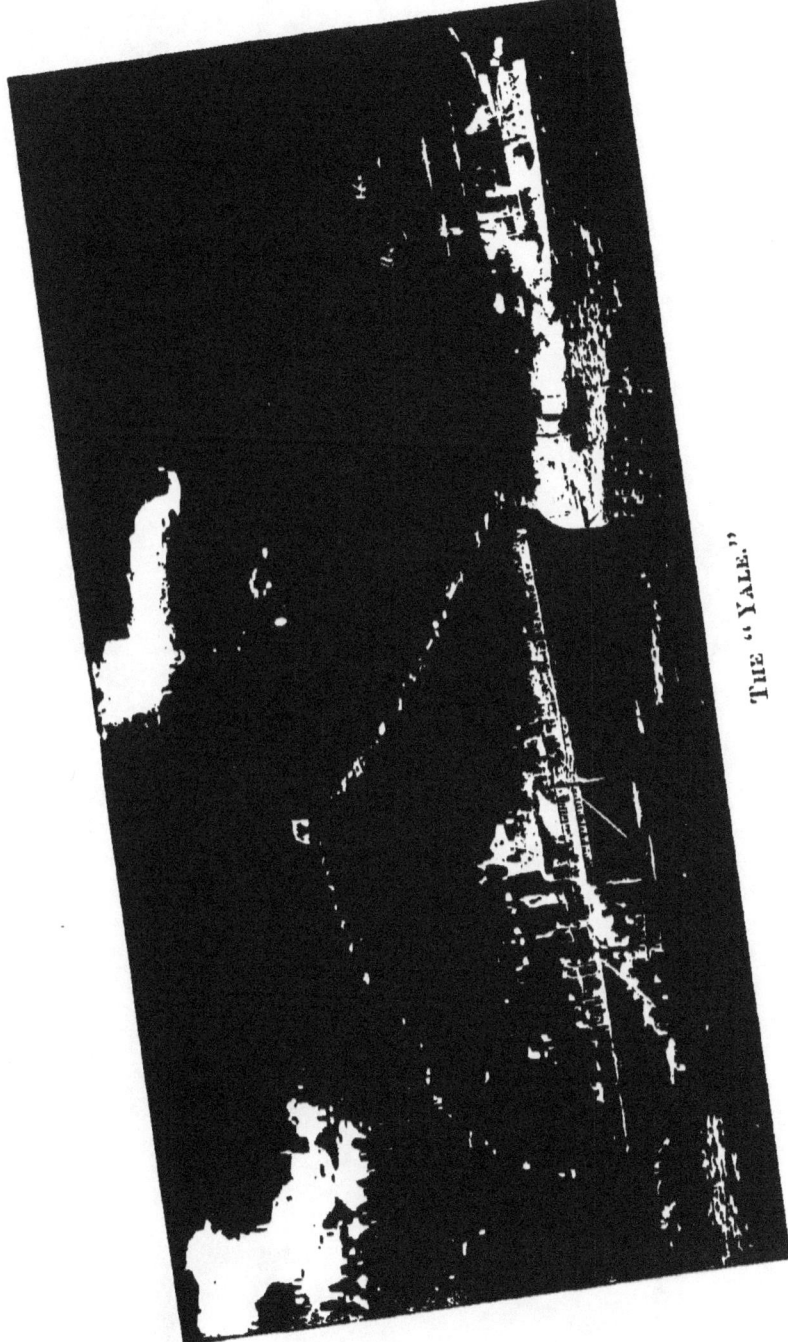

The "YALE."

off Morro Castle and heard the dull boom of the guns, as it came to us across the water, the excitement among the men showed it was the message they had been waiting to hear. It was the end of the bombardment of Santiago by the fleet, as it had found the range of the city and was waiting for land operations to proceed before bombarding again.

About noon we arrived off Siboney, and reported to the "New York," and Admiral Sampson came on board and was closeted with General Miles for half an hour, when the final plans for the strategic move of the combined forces of the army and navy were arranged.

General Miles afterwards went ashore, landing at Siboney, when in a very short time the flames rising from the row of houses signalled the message to the fleet that it did not require a code to translate, of the prevalence of Yellow Jack. The village was burned under the supervision of Dr. Greenleaf of Boston, by General Miles's order. When the General returned to the "Yale" his worried expression told how anxious he was regarding the fever ashore, and the possibility, if the Spaniards held out, of our having a worse foe to contend with than Spaniards.

On the tenth of July we were ordered to turn in our blue uniforms, as we were wearing the brown canvas suits, and there was every reason to believe that we would soon be in a position on shore where we would want no superfluous belongings. On the 12th General Miles again went on shore, and Colonel Woodward was informed that the regiment would be landed in a small bay on the west side of the city, to take Sacopa battery, and then join the right wing of the army. The next morning, however, the truce was still on, and the landing was postponed. The next day we were given three days' rations and ordered to prepare to land the following morning. The men knew what it meant, as the fate of the regiments in Cuba was well known, but there was not a waver or sign of regret or fear. The evening of the 13th men spent in writing letters home which they thought might be their last, and in talking quietly in groups, or in some cases singing hymns. On the other hand there was the element that tried to hide all feelings of seriousness, and to cover any expression of feeling by bravado talk, even offering wagers as to "who would get there first." A seriousness that can be joked about now pervaded the entire boat, and men lay down to sleep with visions of New England homes more vividly impressed than usual on their memories. That night the signal was flashed from shore that we were to advance the following day and take the Sacopa battery on the west side of Morro Castle, thus completing the circle about Santiago.

There is no doubt the arrival of General Miles with the transports in the harbor of Siboney, and the view of these from Morro as we steamed slowly in full view of her glasses had an undue importance in the final decision of the surrender of Santiago, as the news of the arrival of an apparently large force of men waiting on deck in heavy marching order was signalled from Morro to Santiago, confirming General Miles's argument to the officials that he had an unlimited supply of men ready to land and that it would be better for his terms to be accepted with the transportation of the Spanish troops to Spain than for them to await the inevitable overpowering and lose that advantage.

When the hour of expiration of the truce passed and the white flag still told of a continued conference, and possible peace without our landing, the discontent of the men was marked; and when the signal finally came that "Santiago has surrendered," the cheers and jollification was for another American victory, and not a rejoicing at having escaped the dangers of Cuba; for it was a great disappointment to have been so near and an eye witness, yet "not to have been in at the death."

OFF MORRO CASTLE

"The shrill whistle of a boatswain's mate followed by the nasal drawl of a sailor's voice calling the Port Watch to dinner, broke the monotonous stillness on the decks of the United States cruiser 'Yale.'

"The 'Yale,' swinging lazily in the blue waters of the Caribbean Sea, lay about halfway between the Spanish stronghold, the Castle of Morro, and the town of Siboney. Her decks were crowded with soldiers of the 6th Massachusetts and 6th Illinois, who lay sleeping or smoking, and vainly trying to keep out of the terrific heat of the sun.

"With the boatswain's whistle a few got up and lounged over the hot decks towards the 'forward companion-way' that led to the sailors' mess. Here they waited, while the sailors ate their piping hot dinner, with a half-hearted hope that some of the well-fed Jackies, who strolled so contentedly up the gangway still licking their chops, might have a bit of bread stowed away under their white shirts; but their patience went unrewarded, so they lounged back again towards their respective company quarters to be in readiness for the mess call that would soon sound for them. In a few minutes they got their gill of coffee and their mouldy hardtack, which, with the fatty salt pork they got. they made into greasy sandwiches, and climbing upon the rail they munched away at their unappetizing meal and drearily watched the ships of war that lay about them.

"Just abreast of the 'Yale' lay the 'Columbia,' the water sizzling with the heat as it sprayed against her iron prow. Astern of her drifted the old 'Massachusetts' with the front of her turrets and fighting mast white with saltpetre, and the red lead showing through her gray war paint like blood. In the distance could be seen the 'New York,' the 'Oregon,' the 'Texas,' and many other ships of battle.

"Off the port bow and not five miles away, the Castle of Morro stood like an ancient warrior, keeping solitary vigil on the long, high ridge of land that hides Santiago from the sea. Above the castle floated a white flag of truce.

"Behind the fort was Santiago, backed by the high hills of Cuba, and surrounded by Shafter's army. Suddenly, a dozen different colored pennants fluttered to the mast-head of the 'New York.' Instantly half a dozen glasses were levelled at them from the bridge of the 'Yale,' where army and navy officers gathered to catch the order.

"'Form line of battle to attack Morro and bombard Santiago,' it read. The armistice would be up at two o'clock and it then lacked fifteen minutes of two.

"Slowly the great ships swung into line. From every bridge signals were being wig-wagged in rapid order. Everywhere decks were being cleared for action. The little 'Gloucester' crept away in shore and steamed cautiously up in the direction of Morro.

"On the 'Yale,' sailors sprang to their stations, marines manned the several guns, and coolly awaited the order to 'fire.' Soldiers sought good positions from which to observe the fun, although the boats, heavily loaded with ammunition and rations, and swinging out over the water, told them only too plainly that a part of the work would be reserved for them.

"Five minutes of two, and the semi-circle of ships around Morro was formed. Slowly the minutes crept along, and the circle grew smaller and smaller. Two minutes of two and the little 'Gloucester' seemed right under the very guns of the castle. Breathlessly the white flag over Morro was watched. In one minute it must come down. In one minute every silent ship and the silent fort would be wrapped in great, yellow clouds of smoke from which vivid flashes and deafening crashes would follow one another in quick succession.

"After what seemed hours, the ships' bells rang out the hour.

"Minute after minute went by, while the ships lay motionless and silent.

"Presently it was discovered that the 'New York' was wig-wagging to some one on shore. Following along the line of beach the eye came to the bridge on the Siboney railroad, where the 'Michigan' turned and ran under the fire of the guns of Morro. Then a little to the left of the bridge a white flag with a red spot in the centre wig-wagged the message, 'General Toral has surrendered Santiago and the whole of Western Cuba.'

"No sooner had the message been finished than a mighty cheer arose from the 'New York.' Soon the sailors and soldiers were wildly cheering the joyful news. With the breaking up of the battle line ships went steaming rapidly away down the coast, and night, when it shut darkly down around the 'Yale,' hid only two or three ships off Siboney, and the castle of Morro unguarded and unwatched with the white flag still floating in the air.

"BRAINERD TAYLOR."

General Miles did not come on board again until the surrender was announced, when we ran back to Guantanamo, where we anchored in the harbor among a fleet of some twenty war-ships and transports, forming a floating city, the population of which was increased each day by the arrival of some new vessel.

From the 14th to the 17th, the " Yale " made her daily trips up the coast, returning to Siboney every night. On the 17th came the formal surrender of the city, and the same day the " Yale " started for Guantanamo, where she anchored. The " Rita," a prize steamer, with the 6th Illinois on board, also arrived at Guantanamo the same day, and Colonel Foster paid a visit to the officers of the 6th Massachusetts.

The hulls of our battleships lay on the water like great, dark birds, swinging lazily with the tide, and only seeming to waken at night when the electric lights would shine out from all sides, outlining their hulls in the darkness and reflecting long darts of light in the dark water beneath, while now and then a search-light would fall meteor-like over the scene, wrapping all in its brilliancy for a moment and then as suddenly disappearing. No theatre ever produced as picturesque a stage setting as the scene which lay daily before us, or as true a representation of diplomatic life as when General Miles would pay a formal visit on board the " Oregon " or the " Massachusetts," and the massive shell-proof decks of those vessels would lend themselves to an afternoon reception of white-ducked officers, while the very rise and fall of the boat on the swell seemed to be in unison with the music of the band, heard faintly over the water from the forward deck.

Such was the variety of scene and action for the early days on the "Yale." But after the excitement attendant on the expected landing and anticipated battle had passed, the natural reaction came,

ON BOARD THE "YALE."

and the tension of nerves relaxed, and men were hungry and thirsty. Quartered on deck, exposed to the rain and wind of a tropical climate, under a burning sun by day and in dampness by night, the men were at the mercy of a treacherous climate at the worst season of the year. Part of the deck was covered by awnings and others were put up at the end of a week. These served the double purpose of protection from heat and rain and to catch water, which was considered a luxury for drinking, as that provided on the boat was distilled, and drawn from a faucet at either end of the ship at a temperature that was sickening hot. When one wanted a drink, it was necessary to line up and drink in turn from a chipped-edged enamel cup that was used in common by the sick and the well. The writer was threatened with arrest by the marine guard for pouring water into his own cup to drink. No canteens were allowed to be filled, which prevented cooling the water even to the temperature of the air. When it rained at night the men would get up off the deck and roll their belongings in their ponchos and shiver in groups until the storm would pass over, and then lie down again on the wet deck. One man who slept near a tap for the hose, and from which the water bubbled up alarmingly near, spoke of it as his "spring bed."

Our meals consisted of coffee, of which we never had enough and that without sugar, hardtack, occasionally fat bacon but usually raw tomatoes, a can of which would be given to two or three men for their dinner, and which at times had passed their day of possible usefulness and were thrown overboard. As an occasional luxury, half-cooked "sow belly," which would have been excellent fare for an Arctic expedition, was served, but this usually went to feed the fishes. The sailors' food was far superior to that of the regiment. Their sympathy was aroused for the men to the extent that they gladly shared their meals whenever possible, although they paid the penalty by arrest if they were found giving or selling food to the soldiers. The only meal which the writer had on board which could be called by that name was a boiled dinner bought from a stoker, and which made a feast for three. Men who live on Beacon Street grabbed food from the refuse of the officers' table which was being thrown overboard, while Harvard men chased small potatoes down the scuppers with an eagerness which could be explained only by the pangs of hunger. Yet the officers had their hardships, for a naval cadet on board told me one day as a real grievance that he got but one biscuit with his cheese and after dinner coffee.

Those who have stood on deck a steamer looking down at the steerage passengers eating their boiled dinner, or broth from a bucket, with their mugs of beer beside them, and pitied them, pitied a condition that would have been absolute luxury to the men on the "Yale."

The cooking for thirteen companies, thirteen

hundred men, was done in the steerage galley, in a space of not over eight by sixteen feet, the only exception being when as a special favor the use of the second cabin galley was secured during the night for cooking beans.

The letter of E. B. Lamson, under date of August 5, said, "The hardtack was mouldy in hundreds of cases, and was thrown away by soldiers who knew they would get no more to eat for the day. The pork was chiefly fat, which was not suited for food in that climate. No fault was found with the coffee but its scantiness. Many of the privates went a day at a time with nothing in their stomachs but coffee. Now and then they received tomatoes or bean soup. It seemed at times as if the rations were dealt out most sparingly or else there was a most uneven distribution."

One of our men whom the gnawing of hunger drove to the extremity of going to the galley of the first cabin and begging for something to eat was asked, "Are you a waiter?" Upon replying in the negative he was invited to go to a place warmer than the galley, and received no food.

The position of "waiter" was in great demand, as those who had been fortunate enough to secure such a place received plenty to eat, and when possible helped out their friends. The men who had money paid any price for anything they could buy to eat.

Frank Pope writes under the date of July 12:

"The food for the men has been poor; not only poor, but for the last few days rather scarce. They have done considerable kicking about it, but it is partly their own fault. I saw several dozen pieces of hardtack and a lot of canned beef thrown overboard yesterday to coax the sharks nearer the ship.

"Last night we had a terrific rain storm. The rain fell in sheets all night, and everybody on deck was wet through. The men were lying in three or four inches of water, and the baggage was floating off into the scuppers. There was no shelter for them, so they had to grin and bear it. They huddled together under the lee of the deck-house until daylight, when there was a lull in the storm, but it soon started again harder than ever.

"Ponchos were no good. They were soaked through in five minutes, and all woollen blankets and clothing were as bad. The sun came out about noon, however, and dried things off, making everybody feel more cheerful. The clothes and blankets were spread out all over the ship until she looked like a great floating laundry."

The storm here described was perhaps the worst, and as it increased in violence men retreated to the only possible shelter, going to the passage way leading to and in the toilet rooms, where later rows of men sat asleep exhausted beyond wakefulness.

The advantage in waiting until this time to tell the story of the campaign, is that statements concerning food given the regiments are given out from headquarters and do not need verifying.

CLEVELAND, December 30.

General George A. Garretson, of this city, who commanded a division in Porto Rico, agreed to-day with General Miles that the canned beef furnished the army was, to a large extent, unfit for use. He said that a large amount of the meat had to be thrown away.

"The condition of affairs," said General Garretson, "was every bit as bad as is reported. There is no doubt that this bad meat was the cause of a large part of the sickness among the men."

This was some of the "canned beef" that was reported as being wasted by using it as feed to tempt sharks. If the stomach of that fish is anything like a man's, we know what happened to the shark.

> "Near Cuba there lived a young shark,
> Who fed always about some new barque.
> He ate meat from the 'Yale,'
> Then turned up his tail —
> The end of the tale of the shark."

The sanitary arrangements were those accorded the steerage passengers, and were entirely inadequate to the demands of the number of men on board. The only relief to their discomfort was the bath each day when the hose was played on the forward deck, or the evening plunge into the sea, which was allowed for a period of time while lying in the harbor. For exercise we had setting up drill, target practice, and running around the deck, to keep which from being scratched, the men were ordered to take off their shoes and run bare-

A Shower Bath.

foot over a surface that was heated to a temperature that was painful to the touch. It gave the men good knee action, however, and they entered into the sport of the game. This running was finally stopped by General Miles, as the confusion disturbed the work of his staff in his saloon.

Days dragged on into weeks, and the half-starved men, crowded on a transport in mid-summer in the tropics, began to break down with a rapidity which alarmed even the surgeons. The expedition had been sent as a hurried relief to General Shafter, and as it was expected it would be on board the "Yale" but four or five days, provision had been made for that time only. Tons of stores deep down in the inaccessible regions of the hold, and nine cars full of supplies left on the tracks at Charleston, answered admirably to Mr. Hooley's version of Secretary Alger's letter to "Chauncy Depoo," where he says, "In two months I had enough supplies piled up in Maine to feed ivry sojer in Cubea, and all the rig'mints had to do was to write f'r thim."

The second cabin saloon which was utilized as the sick bay was filled to overflowing. Those who looked in through the ports and saw the crowd of naked men panting for air they could not get and calling for nurses when there were none to hear, will not soon forget the sight. Later a ventilator was put into the hospital, which greatly relieved the men.

Such was the life led by the 6th regiment for eighteen days on board the "Yale," and three days on board the train, making a total of twenty-one days during which time the men had been without sufficient exercise, proper food, or drink. The necessary consequence of this showed itself not only on shipboard but later when the men were called upon to make exertions which, had they been in the condition they were at the time of leaving Camp Alger, would have been made with little difficulty.

The brigadier general and the entire regimental staff were in a position to know the life the men were leading, yet there was no improvement or change made. Individually certain officers did all in their power to improve matters, their complaints, however, receiving no response.

That the officers of the regiments were not pampered by too luxurious living at "first cabin" table is also certain. While privileges were theirs, life was made no more attractive to them than "tactics" allow, as being a transport in the wake of the "Massachusetts" and the "Oregon" instead of overhauling rich Spanish vessels, was no doubt aggravating to the "Yale." There were rumors that the supply of coal and tomatoes was low and in danger of being exhausted. The rumor proved false.

During these days General Miles and his staff, together with Captain Paget of the English navy, made their headquarters on board the "Yale,"— the general often appearing on deck in his shirt sleeves for a breathing spell, talking freely and familiarly with any of the men who happened to be near, furnishing a pleasant contrast to some of the lesser lights. Whenever returning from shore the general used the greatest care, and took every precaution of disinfecting before going on board. Others were not as thoughtful. Col. J. J. Astor and Captain Lee succeeded in boarding the "Yale" one evening through the gang being lowered for General Miles. The general had gone to the other side of the ship, however, and in the interim these officers came on board and dined with the army officers before knowledge of their presence reached Captain Wise of the "Yale." Duty called them ashore immediately after the captain learned of their presence, as he did not care to have yellow fever brought aboard by even an officer.

The mail from the North arrived at Guantanamo on the 20th, and a detail was sent from the "Yale" to sort it.

Occasionally one was made to forget the monotonous life we were leading by our unusual environment.

I had been doing guard duty on the "Yale" during the night, and from two to four A. M. had looked out over the harbor filled with the great boats, which were dimly outlined in the starlight, with only here and there a single light shining out in the dark like a wakeful eye over the sleeping forms covering the decks. Entire silence reigned, with the exception of the bells striking the hour, when from one ship, then another, in different tones and keys would come across the water the sound of the ship's bells, like voices of night, bearing the message, "All is well." Eight bells struck, and the arrival of the new guard relieved us. We were just turning for our blankets, to throw ourselves on the deck for an hour's sleep, when, like a ship rising out of the fog, the forms of the fleet about us became dimly visible in the first gray of dawn. They were so unreal as to be truly like phantom ships. Gradually the light increased, not by brightening rays from a rosy dawn, but sombre and dark in color like a November day. Great gray clouds filled the horizon, forming a background so nearly the color of the drab hulled ships that they became part of one another. The light increased, and the water reflected the tint of the sky. It was a monochrome picture such as would fill the heart of an artist with delight. But a sadness pervaded the scene as though Nature had gone into second mourning.

Long after the heat of day had dissipated those soft colors and brought into bold relief every outline of our floating city and its restless population, did the remembrance of that picture fill my mind, and make me forget for the time the horrors of the "Yale."

At an early date in the war the conquest of

the island of Porto Rico had become a settled purpose of the administration. The invasion had been deferred from time to time for reasons connected with the Santiago campaign, and wishing to use the experienced regiments engaged in Cuba. Yet the occupation of this island, owing to its intrinsic value as well as its strategic use, was held to be indispensable before the conclusion of the war. It was planned to send an army to Porto Rico large enough to effect a rapid conquest, and it took time to get the proper forces together. Major General Miles, Commander-in-Chief of the expedition, was ready to sail with our troops from Cuba on July the 18th, but the delay which occurred owing to tardiness of Admiral Sampson in furnishing a requisite naval escort, kept us on the "Yale" until the 25th of July. To complete the expedition, large bodies of troops were to be sent from Charleston, Tampa, and Newport News under command of Major General Brooke. When we sailed on the 21st the expedition from Charleston, numbering about three thousand men, was already under way, and fear was entertained of its reaching the place of rendezvous ahead of the naval guard.

General Brooke with over five thousand men left Newport News a week later. These were to be followed by other forces until the expedition should number about thirty-five thousand men. Quantities of supplies were sent with the troops, who were accompanied by a large number of engineers equipped with all necessary engineering machinery for road and bridge building.

The reasons for keeping the regiment on board the "Yale" so long are thus explained. After the surrender of Santiago there was every reason why no landing should be made in Cuba, and the unexpected delay in the completion of the Porto Rican expedition extended day by day the time into weeks before the plans were completed and the word given to proceed.

It was with cheers of delight that the regiment hailed the positive announcement that we were to move against Porto Rico, as on the 21st day of July the fleet, consisting of sixteen vessels, moved slowly out of the harbor at Guantanamo with the "Massachusetts" as flagship, followed by the "Yale," the "Dixie," "Columbia," and "Gloucester," and the transports "Lampasus," "Comanche," "Rita," "Unionist," "Stillwater," "City of Macon," "Nueces," and "Specialist," carrying about thirty-five hundred men. A low rate of speed was necessary owing to the transports being unable to keep up with the cruisers. The expedition was in charge of Captain Higginson, and during the days of the voyage every sail sighted was overhauled so there was no possibility of our approach being heralded. On the morning of the 23d, Corp. Charles F. Parker died, and was buried at sea the same day. Chaplain Dusseault read the burial service, and a squad of twelve men fired the customary three volleys.

Lieutenant Higginson of General Miles's staff had previously made a journey incognito at great

THE HARBOR OF GUANICA.

risk through Porto Rico, and familiarized himself with the island and its harbors, including the little harbor of Guanica. General Miles, taking advantage of this knowledge, decided to land his forces there instead of on the north side of the island, as was anticipated. He, therefore, sent the "Dixie" to warn General Brooke at Cape San Juan, and changed the course of the fleet southward through the Mona passage. All through the night previous to our landing, as the fleet steamed slowly down the west end of the island, but a single light showed from the entire fleet, and that from the stern of the flagship.

Just before reaching Guanica, General Miles called the officers of the 6th into the main saloon and told them: "There was great work cut out for them; that the most honorable position was theirs, but also the post of greatest danger. The regiment was to force a landing and hold it against every assault until reinforcements arrived, and he hoped they would go forward against everything without flinching."

When the citizens of Guanica wakened on the morning of July 25th, it was to find their town, if not its citizens famous, with our fleet at their doors. They had a garrison of but fifty men, and no communications by rail or wire with any centre where it was possible to secure aid in time to prevent troops landing. The "Gloucester," in command of Lieutenant-Colonel Wainwright, regardless of possible mines, ran boldly into the harbor, where after reconnoitring, she lowered a launch in which were taken thirty men and a Colt rapid-fire gun under the command of Lieutenant Huse, who landed without opposition. Not until the Spanish flag, which floated from a staff at the little wharf, was hauled down and the stars and stripes were run up in its place, did he draw the fire of the Spaniards, from their hiding-places behind houses. The fire was returned, and then, as a number of Spanish cavalry were seen to be hastening to the relief of their comrades, began "that hideous bombardment of the 'Gloucester's' three pounders," dropping shells in such a position that the Spanish cavalry decided discretion to be the better part of valor, and retreated. The troops were landed by aid of the small boats and the "City of Macon," on board which the 6th Massachusetts was taken ashore with General Miles, when it was learned that four of the Spaniards had been killed in the affray, and the others, wishing "to fight another day," had followed the injunctions of the other line, with a promptness that was exhilarating. Not a person was to be seen. Houses were closed, the inhabitants having taken refuge on the hillsides. The regiment was camped near the village, and all possible speed was used in getting horses and artillery ashore.

The captain of the "Macon" was most hospitable, doing double service. When he was on deck with General Miles a certain amount of hospitality was — you could hardly say dispensed —

"acquired" is perhaps the better word, from his stateroom by thirsty privates. They appreciated it just as much as though it had been at the invitation of the captain.

Washington, July 27, the War Department last night received the following:

ST. THOMAS, July 25, 9.35 P.M.

SECRETARY OF WAR, WASHINGTON:

Circumstances were such that I deemed it advisable to take the harbor of Guanica first, fifteen miles west of Ponce, which was successfully accomplished between daylight and eleven o'clock. Spaniards surprised. The "Gloucester," Commander Wainwright, first entered the harbor, and met with slight resistance; fired a few shots. All the transports are now in the harbor, and infantry and artillery rapidly going ashore. This is a well-protected harbor. Water sufficiently deep for all transports and heavy vessels to anchor within two hundred yards of shore. The Spanish flag was lowered and the American flag raised at eleven o'clock to-day. Captain Higginson, with his fleet, has rendered able and earnest assistance. Troops in good health and best of spirits. No casualties.

MILES,
Major General Commanding Army.

CHAPTER V

GUANICA

"When first under fire an' you're wishful to duck,
Don't look nor take 'eed at the man that is struck,
Be thankful you're living and trust to your luck,
And march to your front like a soldier."

JULY 25. It was not far from 9 P. M., well after darkness, that a staff officer of General Garretson rode in from the Yauco road and reported that the company of the 6th Illinois on outpost duty had been fired upon and reinforcements were needed. Lieutenant Colonel Chaffin, being in command of the regiment in the absence of Colonel Woodward, ordered Major Darling to select two companies and go to reinforce the Illinois company. Taking companies L of Boston and M of Milford, he hurried along the road bordered with tropical trees and plants, to where, through a gateway, a path led to the hill on the right on which the Illinois company was posted. Under the guidance of a native guide the surrounding country was reconnoitred and outposts were placed in all available points supposed to be facing the enemy. During the night as the desultory shooting continued and an attack was supposed to be intended by the Spaniards at daybreak, it was deemed advisable to have reinforcements from the camp. Word was sent back to this effect. About one o'clock five companies, A, C, K, G, and E, formed quickly and quietly and marched out to the vicinity of the other companies, to where there was a banana grove on the left at the fork of the road. Beyond this on the left was a hill about three hundred feet high, covered with chaparral, which was recorded as being free from the enemy. The hill terminated at a distance of about four hundred yards, opening out into a large valley to the north. The companies were halted in the rear of this division and consultation was held with General Garretson and staff while waiting for daylight.

July 26. At a little before 5 A. M. the companies were advanced to the outposts at this hollow in the road, where A and G were ordered to lay their rolls in a pile to be left in the charge of a sentinel. Company L was withdrawn from outpost duty, and following in the rear of Company A, which formed the advance guard, was followed by Company G. Only two companies, A and G, were ordered to move up at this time. Company A immediately took up the advance guard formation and started forward. They had proceeded but a few hundred yards when they and the column were fired upon from the side of the hill on the left at a distance of not over two hundred yards. The first volley caused a little confusion in the ranks, but the men quickly recovered from any demoralization. Captain Gihon of Company A was shot in the thigh, Corp. W. S. Carpenter of Company L and B. Bostic, Private, in the arm and finger. Private J. Drummond of Company K was struck twice, the first ball passing completely through the neck near the spinal cord; but Private Drummond refused to fall back and proceeded with the firing line, when he received the second wound, which drew blood but proved to be only a flesh wound. Company C followed Company L. Companies K and E being in under fire broke at first but quickly rallied and pushed to the left and up the hill to the front.

The companies in the road, A, L, and C, jumped into the ditches on either side of the road at the first discharge. As was afterwards learned, the position held by the Spaniards at a distance of not over two hundred yards away, commanded the ditches on both sides of the road. That no more men were wounded can only be explained by the Spaniards having fired five rounds from their hips and then running. The over shooting was shown by the fact that the majority of the wounds were received by the men who were in the rear. On the right of the road was a barbed wire fence and a banana grove, which in the early morning was very black, but through which the flankers of the advance guard and companies pushed. The flankers on the left side of the hill had not reached more than one third of the way up the hill and were within one hundred and fifty yards of the enemy when the Spanish ambuscade opened fire. That portion of the enemy, after firing from the hill-top, retreated over the other side of the hill to the left and north and did not again come into sight.

The shots fired by the 6th Illinois, who were stationed at a house on the hillside a quarter of a mile to the right and rear, came so uncomfortably near to the 6th Massachusetts men that they were called upon to cease firing. The firing did not last over three quarters of an hour. Company A, when getting up on the hillside to the left of the road, could see the Spaniards lying down in a cornfield to the front and right, and fired upon them, to the surprise of those in front of them down in the road, from whom the Spaniards were concealed. The Spaniards retreated down the road, pausing in a sugar mill under cover of a French flag, half a mile away. Another body of Spaniards could be seen on the hillside across the valley retreating to the north. The line advanced down the road until they emerged to the east of the hill-top where the ambuscade took place, and halted along the base of the hill which stretches to the north in line of skirmishers. After pausing there a moment to get breath, they moved out across the ploughed ground toward the sugar mill through a field green with the growth of young sugar-cane plants. By this time Captain McNeely with eighteen of his company came over the hill and took up a position on the left, as skirmishers on the line to the left of K (E, K, G, and part of C to the left of the road). After resting for a while at the foot of the hill, the line moved out to the sugar mill simultaneously, from which they found the enemy had retreated without being fired upon. On the left side of the road the line moved to the front a quarter of a mile to where the valley opened into the next one. Those in the valley waited until three companies on the left hand mounted the next spur separating the valley. When they reached the top of the hill, the enemy was seen drawn up in columns of four on the side of a spur across the valley running parallel to the first one. The enemy were in three or four columns, and could also be seen from the valley. The company on the hill-top commenced to fire on the enemy when orders came from General Garretson down the road to retire.

After the first fire at the enemy, Lieutenant Langhorn called for volunteers to clear the hill, when Second Lieut. F. E. Gray of Company A stepped forward and with the first three fours of his company advanced up the hill and accomplished what was desired.

An extract from a letter from a man who was under fire for the first time says: —

"At the first volley I was simply surprised. I instinctively dropped on my stomach beside the road, keeping my head up to get a chance to shoot. During that terrible storm I felt as if I had been in the same position many times before. I did not have the slightest tremor. About six I was lying beside Captain Gihon talking about the battle, with bullets flying thick and fast on three sides, when he groaned and dropped his head. Then my heart jumped and I said, 'Are you hit, captain?' He said 'Yes.' I asked him where. He laughed and said, 'In the seat of my pants.' We found that a Mauser bullet had passed through his left hip. It must have passed over my head, and frightfully near. The captain stayed through the battle in command."

To those left in camp the night had been one of suspense and excitement. During the entire night desultory shots had been heard from all sides, but principally from the direction the troops had gone. About day-break the sound of continuous heavy firing told of conflict begun in earnest. Rumors of terrible disaster soon filled the camp, and the word was given out by a high regiment official that one company was entirely wiped out and another had suffered great loss. Captain Barrett appeared wounded by a bad cut from the barbed wire fence. The blood covering his face and filling his eyes, necessitated his coming to camp to have his head dressed, after which he returned to his command. Shortly after this Captain Gibon was brought in to the hospital, and the appearance in the road immediately after of a large number of natives following stretchers confirmed the impression that our surgeons would be kept busy. Every effort was being made to care for a large number of wounded, when the good news arrived that only three were wounded of all our men, causing great rejoicing throughout the camp.

The men who went for outpost duty that first night, it must be remembered, did so in an enemy's unknown country with no knowledge of the "lay of the land," taking their position after darkness had fallen and with no idea of the number of the enemy that might be collected on their front. That men who had never before been under fire, should have held their ground during the night as they did, is deserving of all praise.

Major Darling after consultation with Lieutenant Langhorn located the companies and remained in charge of the post until the arrival of the reinforcements, when General Garretson took charge.

Adjutant Ames, who was conspicuous throughout the fight, appeared to the men in a new light. The quiet manner of camp became under fire one of fearlessness and bravery that called forth the highest admiration from the men.

It was expected during the entire day that the Spaniards would make another attack the following night, and preparations were made to give them a warm reception. There was no opportunity of getting food to the men, and they worked all day with nothing but hardtack and water to sustain them, throwing up trenches and whatever form of defence was possible. Toward night word came of the scarcity of food in the companies, when eleven men of Company A, who had been on guard duty the night before, volunteered to take coffee up to their company. Buckets full were soon prepared, and the squad started out in command of Corporal Richardson. Before the outskirts of the village were passed, night had fallen. The men proceeded, however, over a road bordered on either side with fields of sugar-cane or dense hedges, taking turns in carrying the coffee, and not knowing what minute they might draw the fire of the Spaniards. About a mile out they were halted by a detail of Red Cross men, who directed them to the locality of the company as nearly as they knew. Another mile passed, when they were halted by the outpost of the 6th and were told that Company A was one half-mile beyond upon the hill. They started on, but a moment after were recalled by a messenger sent by Major Taylor, who was in charge of the force in the trenches which they had passed. He feared their being ambuscaded, and detained them in the trenches with his command. Two or three hours later word was received that the road was clear to the company, and part of the detail went on with the coffee, reaching the company without accident, where it is needless to say they were warmly welcomed.

The night in the trenches was spent in needless alarm. About midnight a horse was heard clattering down the hard road, when Lieutenant Langhorn, who had won the admiration of the men the night before by his bravery, appeared. He was greeted with the remark, "Are n't you afraid you 'll be shot, lieutenant?" and replied, "That is what we are paid for." Later Major Taylor was relieved owing to illness and Captain Greig was left as acting major. Morning broke, and the surgeons and their assistants were free to return to camp as there had been no casualties at the front.

MAJOR EDWARD J. GIHON.

PORT PONCE, PORTO RICO, July 28, 1898.
SECRETARY WAR, WASHINGTON:

In the affair of the 26th, Capt. Edward J. Gihon of Co. A was wounded in the left hip, Corp. H. J. Pryor of Co. L slightly wounded in hand; Private James Drummond, Co. K, two wounds in neck, Private B. F. Bostic, Co. L, slightly wounded right arm. All of 6th Massachusetts all doing well.

The Spanish retreat from this place was precipitate, they leaving rifles and ammunition in barracks and forty or fifty sick in hospitals. The people are enjoying a holiday in our arrival. MILES.

General Garretson telegraphed : —

"The following officers of the command are respectfully commended for gallantry and coolness under fire: Maj. C. K. Darling, Capt. E. J. Gihon, who was painfully wounded early in the action and remained in command of the company until it reached camp."

The night following the battle a rumored attack on the camp called all available men into service. Adjutant Ames, who had started to the front on a caisson, was ordered back to take command by General Garretson. The troops marched out half a mile from camp, where they were halted with orders not to proceed unless firing ahead began. At the end of a couple of hours, as no Spaniards materialized the men returned to camp.

A private of Company A writes of the battle:

"It was a curious thing, and one that was not noticed until after the battle, and that was the lack of superior officers at the front. There was no colonel or lieutenant colonel, majors, chaplain, or surgeons, and it has been a joke ever since, especially about our major, who came as far as the outpost, and from that time we saw no more of him. But Adjutant Ames, Captain Gihon, Lieutenants Gray and Langhorn, were in the thickest of the fight, cheering the boys and giving advice."

The experiences of men for the first time under fire were various, and at times amusing. With the coolness of being alone in the woods one man took out his pipe and lighted it, as though the Springfields did not make smoke enough to locate us; another chased his hat down the side of the road, while a third declined to shoot a Spaniard with any gun but his own, and went up and down his company line to find his gun to exchange it.

This being our one battle has given it undue prominence. On the other hand, many of the men during the summer on outpost and provost guard duty were placed in situations where a steady nerve was more difficult than in the excitement of battle. A few evenings after the battle, some of the men from Company I had an experience described by one of them as follows: —

Sergeant George G. King of Company I, Concord, in his letter of July 27th gives the following account of a night attack: —

"About nine o'clock Arthur Armstrong, who was three men below me on the dark road, heard a horse's footsteps near him. The horse single-footed down the road toward Armstrong, but the wood was so dark that he couldn't see anything but the black mass. When the right time came he shouted 'Halt' twice. The horse slowed down, stopped, and getting no answer, Armstrong fired over to scare the rider into saying something. When he heard the gun the horse turned and ran back. I could hear the whole performance, and haven't a doubt but what there was a rider. He sent the story down and waited. At ten they called us in. Just as those of us who were above him were crossing Armstrong's coast, we heard the hoof-beats again way up the road. It was too dark then to see anything, but we waited. The horse stopped almost out of hearing. I told Arthur to come along with me to find out what it was. We knew there was Spanish cavalry around, and that there was nothing to prevent their getting over that road and cutting in behind the outposts if we didn't stop them. We went perhaps a hundred yards and then we heard the sound of half a dozen horses' feet coming at a gallop. I whispered to Arthur to come back and ambush with the others. We had just time. I was nearest the horses, and when the black mass loomed up not twenty feet away I holloaed to halt. They made no pretence of stopping, and I pulled, but my gun missed fire. Just then they were within ten feet and I saw they were riderless. But just at the same time three of the boys fired. I shouted to stop them, but the fun had begun and seven of them emptied their rifles. All the horses but one turned and ran. One was badly hurt and fallen. I told two of the boys to shoot him. Poor fellow! they finished him, and we went in. Our skirmish is quite a joke now, but we have the satisfaction of knowing we did the right thing, and of knowing too, that when the blood gets stirred you forget to be afraid, which is a discovery bringing immense relief."

The abundance and cheapness of mangoes were too great a temptation to be resisted, although warned against them by friendly natives. A prevalence of cracked lips in a short time testified to that danger if nothing worse.

Oranges were occasionally found, but they were still green, while pineapples had just gone by.

The orders that men were to go in no store or building of any kind were given, and a guard stationed at all liquor stores (which in Porto Rico means all stores) saw that this rule was strictly enforced. In spite of this certain men managed to "fall off the water wagon" with a bang.

The day after landing a member of the regiment who had come off the "Yale" ill, went to the surgeons at the division hospital tents and asked for medicine. He was told to drink no coffee and to eat no hardtack or tomatoes. "Drink tea and get some nourishing food" was the prescription given. He was told they had nothing of that kind at the dispensary and was given an order on Captain Ham. The order was presented to Captain Ham and he "O. K.'d" it, and gave the man an order on the supplies on one of the ships in the harbor. Hiring a boat a visit was made to the supply ship, with the result that "no small supplies could be dispensed." Used up and sick, the private dragged himself back to camp, where he met Adjutant Ames. He heard his story and immediately took the man and gave him what he wished from his private stock. Later, West, his servant, appeared at the dog tent where the man was lying, with a quart of hot tea, also from the adjutant's store. The lieutenant colonel has probably forgotten the kindness that day shown a private, but he kept a man out of the hospital, who now returns thanks.

The regiment was moved from its first camp on the 28th to a field a short distance back from the coast during the two days we remained there. When the regiment moved on the 30th Major Priest was left with Companies B and D for guard duty.

CHAPTER VI

RESIGNATION OF OFFICERS AT PONCE

JULY 27. A foothold having been won at Guanica and sufficient forces landed to hold that section, Commander Davis left Guanica with the "Dixie," "Gloucester," "Annapolis," and "Wasp," for the port of Ponce to capture lighters for the use of the United States army. There was no resistance, the Spaniards having evacuated the place, surrendering to Commander Davis on demand, and the American flag was raised on the 28th. Sixty lighters and twenty sailing vessels were found and appropriated. General Miles soon after arrived with the transports conveying General Ernst's brigade, which was landed at once and entered the city amidst great enthusiasm and applause. Harding Davis says "Ponce had the surrender habit," and that it was unsafe for a uniformed man to enter the town if he did not wish to receive an official and unconditional surrender.

General Miles issued the following proclamation:

"In the prosecution of the war against the kingdom of Spain by the people of the United States, in the

NELSON A. MILES,
Major-General commanding U. S. Army.

cause of liberty, justice, and humanity, its military forces have come to occupy the island of Porto Rico. They come bearing the banners of freedom, inspired by a noble purpose, to seek the enemies of our Government and of yours, and to destroy or capture all in armed resistance. They bring to you the fostering arms of a free people, whose greatest power is justice and humanity to all living within their fold. Hence they release you from your former political relations, and, it is hoped, this will be followed by your cheerful acceptance of the Government of the United States.

"The chief object of the American military forces will be to overthrow the armed authority of Spain and give the people of your beautiful island the largest measure of liberty consistent with this military occupation. They have not come to make war on the people of the country, who for centuries have been oppressed. But on the contrary, they bring protection not only to yourselves, but to your property, promote your prosperity, and bestow the immunities and blessing of our enlightened and liberal institutions and Government.

"It is not their purpose to interfere with the existing laws and customs which are wholesome and beneficial to the people, so long as they conform to the rules of the military administration, in order and justice. This is not a war of devastation and desolation, but one to give all the advantages and blessings of enlightened civilization."

July 30. With the 6th Illinois as advance guard, followed by four batteries of artillery, the 6th Massachusetts regiment started from Guanica at 9 A. M., anxious to overtake the retreating Spaniards. With colors flying and enlivened by the martial music of the band we marched through the village, cheered by the natives and the remaining troops. The band played us out of town and again by the trenches and the field where the battle had been fought, and then, well, they had other use for their breath. Were it not a part of the suffering of the regiment, the story of the gradual dissolution of our band from Guanica to Ponce until a bass drum and clarionet were about all the instruments left at the head of the column would be amusing. With the adaptability of Yankees, however, when Ponce was reached a full corps was improvised from our men, and they blew us through the town.

Yauco was reached about 2 P. M., where we received a welcome such as can be shown only in the over-demonstrative temperaments of an excitable people. The enthusiasm, however, here as in all other places was confined mostly to the lower classes, who shouted, danced, yelled, ran after the band, and became fairly insane when it played, it being the first time many of them had ever seen or heard such an organization.

July 31. Yauco was left at 7.30 A. M., and the regiment marched ten miles to Tallaboa.

Major Darling returned to Yauco when the regiment left Tallaboa the following day, where Company L had been left on provost duty, and gave the citizens their first lesson in the method of United States administration. Dr. Gross remained there also in charge of the hospital, with fifty-two of our sick men.

Extract of letter of private, Company L: —

"... On July 30 our brigade left Guanica and marched eight miles to Yauco, which is quite a nice little place.

SPANISH BLOCK-HOUSE.

We camped there over night, and early the next morning the rest of the push all started except Company L. which was left behind to garrison the town for a while. We had an ideal camp ground on the hillside, and the surrounding view was grand, — large sugar-cane fields, cocoanut-trees, banana-trees, mangoes, and coffee. It was immense, and the mountains all around, and with the weather we had this life was like a dream. On our right was the town, back of us was the edge of a precipice, and to our left down the hill was a winding river, and all spread out in front of us was this splendid view. Major Darling stayed with us and acted as mayor of the town, and Lieutenant Jackson was his assistant.

NATIVE LAUNDRY.

Every morning numbers of women and girls would pass along the road in front of the camp down to the river to wash clothes. They squat along the banks, washing the clothes on the stones, beating them with a flat stick, and the clothes they wash are white and clean as can be. The majority of the natives are pretty destitute, and if it wasn't for the sugar-cane would starve, as they are eating sugar-cane all the time. Hardtack is a great luxury for Yauco. The natives brought us everything we wanted, and I used to get my washing done in ex-

H. W. GROSS,
First Lieutenant and Assistant Surgeon.

change for a few hardtacks. There are lots of pretty girls here and lots of ugly ones, just like any other place. Our company was ordered from Yauco August 5th to join our regiment at Ponce, so that afternoon we were taken to Ponce on a freight train about twenty-three miles."

August 1. Just after leaving Tallaboa, we passed a house where two ladies from the piazza of their house were watching the troops. One with snow-white hair held out her arms and raised her eyes to the heavens in a prayer of quiet thanksgiving for the sight. Her dignity and beauty made one feel she was saying, " Mine eyes have seen the glory of the coming of the Lord." It was one of the few cases of the well-to-do showing enthusiasm. Many of the best houses we passed were closed and every blind drawn, although occasionally a pair of eyes through a lattice would indicate that there was Spanish curiosity within. One royalist, and she looked it, as she sat on her piazza embroidering, refused to raise her eyes, although living in a secluded place where any excitement would have been welcome. Her servants, however, from the coffee plantation adjoining quite atoned for the seeming indifference of the mistress.

It was on this march that Captain Ham, overtaking a wagon stuck in the mud, asked in the vernacular of Chimmie Fadden, what they were doing.

Receiving a reply he then inquired why there were only three wagons instead of four, commenting, "Just like those d—d volunteers." He then proceeded to lighten the load by pitching boxes of ammunition off the wagon until he came to a box which, as it looked neither like canned tomatoes or ammunition, he was unable to account for. Inquiring what it was, the "L" man replied, "That is the 'articifer's' box." "Articifer, articifer," repeated the captain, "and what in the h—l is an articifer?"

When the regiment left Guanica for Ponce, the men were in heavy marching order, which meant besides their guns and cartridge belts, a canteen, haversack with rations and fifty extra rounds of ammunition, their rolls wrapped in half a shelter tent with blanket, poncho, and tent stakes, and every personal article owned by the soldier, the total weight of all exceeding forty pounds. On no march made by the regiment was the distance covered in one day in excess of what a well man could walk in this climate. But without exception the marches made by the regiment were through the middle and heat of the day, on roads rocky, sandy, or muddy which led over mountains, or through valleys where the sun beat down with merciless rays, between forests, where every breath drawn was like air of an over-heated conservatory on a summer's day. The day's march often started by fording a river, when the men's shoes would be filled with water which soon blistered their feet, so that at the end of two or three hours' walking became agony, when shoes would be taken off and every experiment from

FIVE MINUTES' REST.

going barefooted to the primitive sandal would be tried as a relief. Men whose blood had been exhausted, whose vitality had been lost from starvation, and who told too plainly the story of their suffering in the drawn faces and sunken eyes, taxed beyond their strength, would fall beside the road, too weary to know what was said or to care what was done. Everything that was not absolutely necessary, and in many cases articles that were, including sometimes parts of blankets and even ponchos, were thrown away, in order to lighten their loads.

These were men from one of the best regiments in an army of volunteers of whom it was said: —

"Far more offered indeed than the government was ready to accept, and a most rigid system of health inspection was inaugurated in order that none but those in a state of full health and capable of enduring the hardships of campaigning in a tropical island should be enrolled. The result was to give the government one of the most physically perfect armies that had ever been put in the field."

When a halt was made for a few minutes' rest the ever-present native would go up a cocoanut-tree with a rapidity and dexterity that would shame a monkey. As the nuts were dropped one at a time a general scramble would take place for them, the lucky winner carrying off his prize to another native, who with one stroke of his deftly handled machete would open the end and place the coveted milk in reach. No champagne ever equalled the sparkle and thirst-quenching property of the cocoanut milk on those marches.

As in all large bodies of men there is a percentage of sickness from indiscretions of life or diet, so such existed in this regiment. Lack of nourishing food stimulated a desire for drink, and the difficulty of obtaining water on the marches made men, when seized with the terrible hunger and thirst attendant on exertion in the tropics, not only careless but desperate in their disregard of sanitary laws.

There were also exceptional cases when men took advantage of the opportunity to fall out in order that they might get in the stores of the town before going to the camp for drink. But day after day boys and men fell by the roadside, whose faces were purple and whose breathing were spasmodic gasps for breath; others in dead faints and some in convulsions, shrieking like maniacs for the water they could not have, left by the roadside with some comrade, to follow on as best they could or to be picked up by the ambulance or surgeons, while the main line pushed forward with the speed of a forced march.

AFTER COCOANUTS.

The feelings of the regiment can perhaps be easier imagined than described, when after all it had endured, such articles as the following editorial from the Baltimore "Sun" of August 6, began to reach camp.

Historic Regiments.

"The 6th Massachusetts was received on its recent passage through Baltimore with great enthusiasm, and some of our municipal officials are said to have wept in the exuberance of the glorious emotions stirred by the sight of it. It has since distinguished itself in a sinister way. When paid off the other day it made a discreditable row. Being sent afterward to Porto Rico, its members lagged behind on the march toward San Juan in a manner the reverse of gallant. All its regimental officers but one are said to have resigned. Its record is on a par with that of the 71st New York, reported by General Kent as having obstructed the advance of his men in the fight before Santiago by lying down so persistently that Kent's men had to march over their prostrate forms. The present 6th Massachusetts seems to be of the class of warriors that win their glory before the fighting begins. Its predecessor was most famous for what it suffered from Baltimore brickbats."

"Et tu, Brute!"

The question is often asked since our return, "Did the men fall out in such numbers?" Yes, they did, not only from the 6th Massachusetts and other volunteer regiments, but also from the regulars. Men who had been starved, or dieted, if you please, until all reserve strength had gone, and were then expected to do the work of strong men, simply could not. Nearly a month had passed since the regiment had received food that was sufficiently nourishing for a working diet, and the result was what might have been expected. The blame for falling out, if blame there be, belongs not to the enlisted men, but to whoever or whatever was responsible for allowing such a condition of affairs to arise, or still more to continue to exist.

That a large percentage of the general sickness which afterwards rendered over half the regiment unfit for duty is due to this same cause of weakened constitutions being more susceptible to disease, there can be no doubt. That there was also a moral influence working unconsciously against discipline and self-control from a loss of confidence in their officers' ability to rectify wrong, after the experiences the regiment had been through on the "Yale," is entirely probable.

IN HEAVY MARCHING ORDER.

TO A. L. K.

When the order "forward" was given,
And the column stretched out and marched
Over roads that were rough and unfinished,
Through forests all burned and parched;
With their rolls, at the first all too heavy,
Increasing as hours dragged away,
But some carried a burden far greater
That could not be thrown off with the day.

A burden of memories vivid,
Burned into the soul with God's fire,
Of life's opportunities wasted
Through failings and weakness so dire,
Which daily grew brighter and brighter
Like iron made ready to bend,
Being heated and hammered and shapen
By God's blacksmith, the judgment of men.

And when the day's journey had ended,
And men threw their burdens aside,
To lie down aweary and slumber
Like boats resting light on the tide;
Then the burden was felt in its fulness,
Relieved from the physical pain,
As through weary nights tossed the soldier
On the endless march in the brain.

For if nature through over-exertion
Claimed the physical man for sleep,
The brain, as though weary of reason,
Rushed backward, fond memories to keep
With those far away from camp turmoil
Amid pleasures uncolored by strife,
To a scene and old friends once familiar,
All dearer — far dearer — than life.

O God, in thy infinite mercy,
Lift this load from a heart-broken man,
Send sleep without dreams to refreshen
The nights now passed under Thy ban,
Till the journey of life gladly ended
We cast down the burden to One,
Who in fulness of knowledge must pity
Such soldiers for sake of Thy Son.

Resignation of Officers 107

August 4. The command arrived at Ponce in the afternoon after a cruel march of twelve miles, presenting a straggling and forlorn appearance, which not even the appeal to "old Glory on the hill" could disguise. United States troops had already taken possession of the city, and as we entered the town  we found among the crowds lining the streets numbers of army and naval officers, immaculate in white duck, "sizing us up." The men were completely exhausted, but they took a tremendous brace, stimulated by our improvised band playing national airs. The reception given the regiment was an enthusiastic one, but the troops were too "done up" to enjoy or appreciate it.

Camp was pitched about two miles beyond Ponce in an old sugar-cane field, rough with furrows and covered with stones, where we had our only experience with centipedes. Scarcely a night passed without Hospital Steward Ryder being awakened to relieve some sufferer, but fortunately, owing to his *peculiarly efficient* treatment, there were no fatal cases.

Up to this time the life of the regiment on the island had been one of such hardship that the eyes of the men had been blinded to the beauties of nature. That we had marched through avenues of cocoanut-trees, along roads bordered with coffee plantations growing in the shadow of banana or orange trees, over mountains whose summits were crowned with royal palms and tree ferns, under precipices of rock festooned with delicate, trailing vines over a groundwork of moss, by rocks whose

A COMPANY STREET.

every crystal seemed to furnish substance for some flowering plant, was obvious to few. With bowed heads and eyes blinded by dust and perspiration, there was no place for beauty. Occasionally a man would reach for an orchid hanging from some wayside rock, or would exclaim on the panoramic view which would open before us as we rounded some sharp curve, where thousands of feet below a stream like a silver ribbon would glisten for a moment in the sun, and then hide itself in its home under the dark foliage. If we passed a brook splashing down over the rocks from its mountain source, it was not the clearness of the water or the sylvan-like haunts in delicate ferns arched over the bed of the brook that was remarked, but the possibility of getting a drink or a canteen filled regardless of the possible typhoid germs ere an order should sound to fall in and not to drink it.

The character and disposition of the natives have been over-estimated and judged entirely too kindly. The enthusiastic reception accorded the troops on all sides in the country and by the crowds in the streets was the expression not of the substantial class of the island but of the crowds always foremost on such occasions in expressing the spirit of the mob, whether it be kindly or threatening; and, while it is of course pleasant to receive a welcome even from the irresponsible class, it is not safe to allow that to stand as the expression of the minds of the intelligent natives. They were like children who, pleased with a new toy or amusement, and dazzled by the uniforms and brass bands, gave over-demonstrative expressions and signs of affection. That this was only ephemeral was shown after a very few weeks, by the diminution of respect felt for and shown the Americans, when the novelty of the situation had worn away and they began to discover that the Americans were not there to entertain them or to enable them to spend the rest of their days in idleness, good-natured

A Group of Natives.

though they be. On the other hand the shopkeepers were not only *not* demonstrative but were in most cases rascally dishonest in their dealings with the very men who were guarding their stores from the violence of the lower classes. Prices were not only increased but in some cases positively doubled over those asked the natives, an abuse which became so great that it became necessary to threaten them with having their stores closed to remedy it. When the troops were paid in Utuado the first time in three months, the men had a large amount of money and spent it freely, even recklessly, when advantage was taken on all sides, both as to rates of exchange and in prices charged.

Those who go to Porto Rico expecting to find a simple-minded, kind-hearted, honest native, will be greatly surprised by the revelation of the true state of affairs. From the children in the market through all classes of tradespeople we found it necessary to be constantly on our guard. Their attitude toward honesty was expressed by one of the leading physicians in Utuado by "We call an honest man a fool down here." That such a state of affairs should exist cannot be wondered at when for years their political system has been in the hands of unscrupulous and money-making officials. "Americano mucho bueno" is pleasant but cheap, and "Americano" will become to the populace "mucho malo" just so soon as Uncle Sam sits down to stay.

No Yankee was ever more keen for business than were the Porto Rican shopkeepers, and the rapidity with which they acquired our trading vocabulary was exceeded only by that of their children. Frequently the small boy who had picked up in a few weeks enough English, acted as interpreter for his less skilful father behind the counter, taking change and learning a new vocabulary at the same time. Children would walk along the street and hold up an article, naming it in Spanish, until you repeated the name of the article in English, when they would go on their way repeating the English word aloud over and over until they could claim it as part of their new vocabulary. Like children they were proud of the new tool, but they invariably wished you "Good-night" at six o'clock in the morning.

I passed one day in the country a small lad walking with his head down on his return from town, and who was all oblivious to the approach of a stranger, so wrapped up was he in his newly acquired English, which he was repeating aloud over and over, "Get to — of here."

August 5. Rumors of disagreement and discontent existing at headquarters were confirmed by the resignation of the three senior officers of the regiment, together with the chaplain and one captain.

The "Boston Journal" gave Massachusetts people the first intimation of trouble in the following despatch:

Colonel Charles Woodward.

FIVE OFFICERS RESIGN.

GREAT SENSATION CAUSED BY TROUBLE IN THE SIXTH MASSACHUSETTS NOW WITH MILES IN PORTO RICO.

BOSTON, Aug. 4.

A special cablegram to the "Journal" from Ponce, Porto Rico, says:

A tremendous sensation has occurred in the Sixth Massachusetts regiment, which is in General Garretson's brigade. The friction between the line officers of the regiment and the officers of the brigade, which has been growing ever since the command left Cuba, reached its climax Monday when Colonel Woodward, Lieutenant Colonel Chaflin, Major Taylor, Chaplain Dusseault, and Captain Goodell of Co. K resigned their commissions.

The exact reason which prompted them to take this action is not at present known.

The resignation leaves Maj. Charles K. Darling in command of the regiment.

The matter has been fully reported to General Miles and a rigid investigation has been ordered. By military law to resign in the face of the enemy means a court-martial.

PONCE, Aug. 7, 1898.

GOVERNOR WOLCOTT:

The resignation of Col. Chas. F. Woodward, 6th Massachusetts, has been accepted to-day, August 5, and I recommend appointment of Lieut. Col. Edmund Rice to fill vacancy. Colonel Rice is here, and I am sure he will make that regiment an honor to the State.

NELSON A. MILES,
Major General Commanding Army.

"GOVERNOR WOLCOTT:

"The colonel and lieutenant colonel Sixth Massachusetts have resigned. I recommend Lieut. Col. Edmund Rice, U. S. Volunteers, who had best regiment in army of Potomac, Nineteenth Massachusetts, be appointed Colonel."

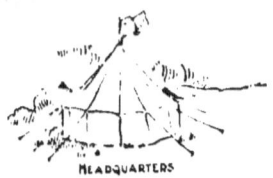
HEADQUARTERS

When the resignation of these officers was accepted, Major Darling, the senior major and next in command, was in charge of affairs at Yauco. Major Priest was engaged in a like duty at Guanica, leaving Captain Cook the senior officer at that time in camp, who acted as colonel until the return, four days later, of Major Darling. Captain Barrett of Company M, who at the same time was the subject of charges of inefficiency, went before the board and was entirely exonerated from any blame, the judgment being that whatever demoralization there had been was the necessary sequence of a disordered condition of affairs at headquarters.

During this unfortunate period, when the regiment was left with no officer higher than a captain in command, the men, if ever inclined to show a spirit of disaffection or demoralization, would have shown it then. No sign of "bad blood" was

MAJOR CHARLES K. DARLING.

manifest. When the news of the resignation of the officers became known, the men gathered in groups and discussed it, but there was no suggestion of breach of discipline.

Before leaving, the lieutenant colonel said good-bye to several companies and was cheered by the men. Individually there were many men in the regiment who for years had known the officers and whose personal feeling was entirely one of kindness.

Chaplain Dusseault was greatly liked by the men, and his departure was regretted by all.

Order was quickly restored by Governor Wolcott's prompt action: —

"Colonel Rice of the regular army was appointed by General Miles to command the regiment, and Adjutant Ames was appointed lieutenant colonel. Major Darling became senior major, Major Priest of the third battalion moved up one point, and Captain Gihon of Company A was appointed acting major of the third battalion.

"In addition to the coming of Col. Edmund Rice as the permanent commander of the regiment, a week later Adjt. Butler Ames was promoted to lieutenant colonel; Lieutenant Gray of Company A to captain, 2d Lieutenant Hunton of Company G to 1st lieutenant, and Sergeant Major Pierson became a 2d lieutenant. The only other two promotions made thereafter in the regiment were of Sergeants Draper and Edwards to 2d lieutenants. Lieutenant Coolidge of Company E became later the permanent regimental adjutant. Captain Gihon of Company A, who, though severely wounded in the skirmish at Yauco road, declined to leave his company during the action, was recommended for promotion; but the War Department's ruling that only two majors were to be allowed to a regiment of infantry in cases where there were not already three, prevented this deserved recognition of his merit. He was, however, commissioned by Governor Wolcott as major, and thereafter commanded a battalion."

Movements of magnitude are usually of necessity slowly put into motion. A pleasing exception to this was the rapidity with which the machinery of the Young Men's Christian Association was got into working order by having, three days after the President's call for volunteers, a meeting of the International Committee of the Y. M. C. Association in the City of New York, when a decision was reached for immediate action. We cannot here go into the history of the wonderful rapidity with which every camp was supplied with a Y. M. C. A. headquarters; suffice it to say it was done, and that without strain or friction in the organization.

Only those familiar with camp life realize what the absence of all places and opportunities for social life means to the soldier. It is hard for him to carry writing materials or to find a place to write his letters. The big tents of the Y. M. C. A. became at once a reading room, writing room, social hall as well as a church. The spirit of tolerance and the atmosphere of brotherhood characterized the headquarters, while the entire absence of sectarianism made all feel equally at home. Second only to the Red Cross society in importance of all organizations connected with our army was the Y. M. C. A.

As an exponent of the best features of this system the men of the 6th Massachusetts were

Mr. Dwight L. Rogers, of the Y. M. C. A.

particularly fortunate in having assigned to them Mr. Dwight L. Rogers, a State Secretary of the Association in Massachusetts. He was with the regiment during the entire summer, and after the resignation of the chaplain, the Rev. Mr. Dusseault, he conducted the Sunday services as well. His uniform devotion to the good of the men, and his sincerity in his untiring efforts to help them in every way, has won for him a place in the hearts of the men that will last as long as the remembrance of the name of Porto Rico.

For reasons known only to those in command at the time there had been no religious services of any kind held in the regiment from July 2d at Camp Alger until August 7th at Ponce, when they were continued by Mr. Rogers. After this date not a Sunday passed without services unless marching.

August 6. The regiment was supplied with new Krag-Jorgensen rifles, when they turned in their old Springfields and part of their extra ammunition.

The first bread we had seen since leaving Camp Alger was found here, and of a quality equal to the best French bread. Milk also was bought from the wagons near the camp.

August 8. Passes were issued for a number of men to go to town, where they were able to get a "square meal" and lay in a supply of tobacco, etc. The French Hotel had not then become so popular but a private could get a table.

Distribution was made in camp of supplies received from the Massachusetts Volunteer Aid Society of pipes, tobacco, canned fruit, and comfort bags.

These last were valued by the men more highly

than anything received, and were retained when everything else was thrown away. The writer still has the one made by No. 62, First Unitarian Society, and hopes the sender of it may some day see this and accept his thanks.

Buttons, patches, rents, were all "attempted" by the men after receiving their "housewives," if the results were not altogether satisfactory.

Whatever formalities are essential to good army discipline were waived on the day when the carriage containing Captain Gihon arrived in camp from Guanica. He had been kept in the hospital there when the regiment left, and no one knew how serious his wound might be. The word of his return as a convalescent spread quickly through the camp, when the carriage was immediately surrounded by the men, who voiced their welcome to the captain in rousing cheers, and demonstrated their affection for him to a degree that made every officer in sight wish he might have been in like position.

General orders No. 19.

Congratulates the officers and men of the Sixth Massachusetts Volunteer Infantry that having had to a greater extent than others of his command an opportunity to show their efficiency under fire they have not failed under the test.

GENERAL GARRETSON.

BOSTON, December, 1898.

Colonel Woodward of the 6th regiment sent his resignation to the governor this morning, and it was immediately accepted.

Col. Charles F. Woodward has been the commanding officer of the 6th regiment, M. V. M., for about eighteen months. When the call for troops was issued last spring, Colonel Woodward was mustered into the United States service and went to Camp Alger, Va., in command of the regiment.

The trouble which culminated in his resignation began at Camp Alger. He incurred the displeasure of Brigadier General Garretson, who commanded the brigade to which the 6th was assigned, by objecting to having Company L, the colored company, removed from the regiment.

General Garretson did not wish to have colored troops in his command, especially as it was only one colored company in a white regiment, and he endeavored to have them transferred to the 9th Ohio colored battalion.

Colonel Woodward, however, objected, and the idea was abandoned.

When the regiment landed in Porto Rico, several complaints were made against Colonel Woodward, alleging that he remained on the transport after his regiment had landed, and did not lead them in the skirmish which took place on the morning after they landed.

The breach between the brigade officers and the regimental officers grew wider, and, finally, when the regiment arrived at Ponce, a board of inquiry was ordered to examine Colonel Woodward and several other officers of the regiment as to efficiency.

The officers thought that this was simply an excuse

to force them out of the service, and, consequently, on August 4, five of them resigned. These five were Colonel Woodward, Lieutenant Colonel Chaffin, Major Taylor, Chaplain Dusseault, and Captain Goodell of Company K.

Although he resigned his commission as colonel of the 6th Massachusetts regiment, United States Volunteers, Colonel Woodward was still colonel of the 6th regiment, M. V. M., and it was this commission that he has resigned to-day.

The law which permitted Colonel Woodward to retain his commission in the Massachusetts Volunteer Militia, after having been commissioned colonel in the United States volunteers, as well as the law creating the provisional militia, was substantially the product of the brain of Colonel Woodward, who at that time was a member of the State Senate, and chairman of the committee on military affairs on the part of the Senate.

Following his resignation from the United States volunteer service and his return home, he reported for duty as colonel of the 6th regiment, M. V. M., much to the surprise of military men.

His resignation, which was accepted to-day, was anticipated, as some eight weeks ago he turned over to the quartermaster general the limited amount of state property in his possession, which is always preliminary to an officer's leaving the service.

When rumors of war began to take the form of probability, Col. Edmund Rice, U. S. A., at that time stationed at Tokio, Japan, asked to be transferred to duty in the United States, where he might be ready for service if war was declared. Thus it happened that when the 6th was left without a colonel, Lieutenant Colonel Rice, being then at Ponce on General Miles's staff, was available for colonel of the 6th Massachusetts, U. S. V. His reluctance to accept this position after application had been made by some of the officers for another colonel explains his delay of several days in joining his command after his appointment.

That the 6th was fortunate, no matter how efficient an officer may have been deprived of promotion by this appointment, no member of the regiment will doubt. Seldom does good fortune favor men in the field as on this occasion. Following the resignation of the regiment's officers, rumors were broadcast as to the demoralized condition of the regiment, until its reputation was in the balance of public opinion. That at this supreme moment such a man as Colonel Rice should have been instantly available did much to save the good name, and prove to the country that the 6th was all right. The after record of the regiment dispelled whatever doubt existed in the minds of the public as to its efficiency, while the following sketch of Colonel Rice's career in army life is a certificate that " the right man to meet the emergency was in the right place."

Colonel Rice was born in Cambridge, Mass., December 2, 1842. He entered the Norwich University in

1856, and remained nearly three years. The degree of B.S. was conferred upon him in 1874 as for 1859.

Captain 19th Massachusetts Volunteers, July 25, 1861.

Engaged in the battle of Ball's Bluff, Peninsular Campaign, battles of Myron's Mills, Siege of Yorktown, West Point, Fair Oaks, Oak Grove, Peach Orchard, Allen's Farm, Savage Station, White Oak Swamp, Glendale (commanded regiment), Malvern Hill, Second Malvern Hill, Bull Run, Fairfax Court House, South Mountain, and Antietam (severely wounded).

Major 19th Massachusetts Volunteers, September, 1862.

Joined regiment at Falmouth, and engaged in the second attack on Fredericksburg, and action at Thoroughfare Gap.

Battle of Gettysburg (wounded twice), in the repulse of Pickett's charge.

Lieutenant Colonel 19th Massachusetts Volunteers, July, 1863. Commanded regiment in the Rapidan campaign of the Army of the Potomac and battles of Bristoe Station, Blackburn's Ford, Robinson's Cross Roads, and Mine Run.

In April, 1864, on the occasion of the review of the different corps of the Army by General Grant, the 19th Massachusetts Volunteers, Lieut. Col. E. Rice commanding, was selected by General Meade, as his was one of the two best-drilled and disciplined regiments in the Army of the Potomac, to drill before Generals Grant, Meade, and Sheridan, and the Corps Commanders.

Commanded regiment in the battles of The Wilderness, 4th, 5th, 6th, and 7th of May; and Spottsylvania,

8th and 9th; Laurel Hill, 10th and 11th. Captured in the assault at the death angle, Spottsylvania, on the morning of the 12th of May, 1864, and in North Carolina, while being conveyed South, escaped by cutting through the door of a freight car in which the prisoners were confined, and jumped from it while the train was under full headway, reached the Union lines, near the Ohio River, after travelling twenty-three nights (resting by day), having walked between three and four hundred miles.

Colonel 19th Massachusetts Volunteers, July, 1864.

Rejoined regiment in front of Petersburg, August, 1864, and in command of Fort Rice, and engaged in the battles of Second Deep Bottom, Weldon Railroad, Ream's Station, and Second Hatcher's Run.

In command of Fort Steadman, and Batteries 11 and 12, in front of Petersburg.

At the surrender of the Rebel Army at Appomattox Court House.

Mustered out June 30th, and regiment disbanded July 20, 1865.

First Lieutenant 40th U. S. Infantry, July, 1866, and received three brevets in the Regular Army, namely:—

Brevet Captain U. S. Army, for gallant and meritorious services at the battle of Antietam, Md.

Brevet Major U. S. Army, for gallant and meritorious services at the battle of Gettysburg, Penn.

Brevet Lieutenant Colonel U. S. Army, for gallant and meritorious services at the battle of The Wilderness, Virginia.

In 1866, was on duty at Camp Distribution, near Washington, D. C.

In February, 1867, ordered to proceed to, and take command of, Fort Caswell, N. C. While *en route*, with troops, on steamer "Flambeaux," was wrecked near the mouth of Cape Fear River.

Ordered to, and in command of, post of Hilton Head, S. C., June, 1868.

Presented by Congress with a medal of honor for leading the advance of his regiment, and the 42d New York, in the charge made to close the gap in our line, and repel Pickett's assault.

"The Congress to Lieut. Col. Edmund Rice, 19th Massachusetts Volunteers, for conspicuous bravery on the 3d day of the battle of Gettysburg."

In the fierceness of this affair, the 19th Massachusetts captured four stands of colors, and lost over one half of its numbers, killed and wounded.

"The conspicuous gallantry of Major Edmund Rice, of the 19th Massachusetts Volunteer Infantry, at the third day's battle of Gettysburg, where he was severely wounded, did more than the single exertion of any other officer on our side to retrieve the day, after the battle had been virtually won by Confederates who had broken our lines, and were cheering and swinging their hats on our captured guns.

"After the line was broken, the 19th dashed in and placed themselves in the rear of the break, and for twelve minutes received the enemy's fire, at a distance of less than fifteen paces. In that time one man in every two of the whole regiment, and seven over, fell, including Rice, who was shot in front of his men, with his foot on the body of a fallen Confederate, he being at that time the officer fighting nearest to the enemy in our whole line. He fought till he fell. His example held them firm at a great crisis in the country's history. He held Pickett's heavy column in check with a single thin line of his regiment, till re-enforcements came from right and left, and thus saved the day."

At the close of the Columbian Exposition, where Colonel Rice was in charge of 4000 soldiers and 86 regular officers, he received the following letter:

WORLD'S COLUMBIAN EXPOSITION,
CHICAGO, March 15, 1894.

COL. EDMUND RICE, COMMANDANT, JACKSON PARK:

SIR, — I am in receipt of your final Report of the Guard and Secret Service of the World's Columbian Exposition. Like every part of your work, this document is admirable. It is orderly, concise, and complete. I shall incorporate it, just as it is, in my own report.

In taking leave of you I must again say what I have so often felt and expressed by word of mouth.

Very soon after I knew you, and from that time on, I placed the deepest confidence in you and depended entirely upon you. Through the great trials, responsibilities, and anxieties of the years we were together, your duties were always discharged with fidelity, and the great interests placed in your hands were conducted with certainty and precision. This is very astonishing, when one recalls the fact that you had but little time in which to organize, and that hundreds of millions of property, and the welfare of hundreds of thousands of people depended upon your skill and attention to duty.

I can only say that there never was an hour in which you were not so keenly alive to every physical condition about you, as to cause comments upon the apparent absence of effort in that direction.

The World's Columbian Exposition owes you a large debt of gratitude, and in its name and my own, I wish to thank you, Sir, for the splendid service you rendered.

Faithfully yours,

[Signed] D. H. BURNHAM,
Director of Works, World's Columbian Exposition.

CHAPTER VII

UTUADO

AFTER the landing of the American troops at Ponce, the arrival of General Garretson's brigade from Guanica led the Spaniards to think that there was but one move anticipated or possible, that being over the military road direct from Ponce to San Juan. Acting upon this supposition, they concentrated their forces at Aibonito, a strong, strategical point in the mountains, where they mined the road for several miles and stored large quantities of explosives in the wayside bushes, making every preparation for a determined stand against the advancing troops.

Instead of attempting this move, General Miles's inception for the campaign was as follows: General Brooke with a force of twelve hundred men went east by boat to Arroyo, on the south shore of the island, from which point he was to march north, intercepting the military road between Aibonito and San Juan, thus cutting off the retreat of the Spaniards toward the latter city. General Schwan marched northwest into the region of Mayaguez,

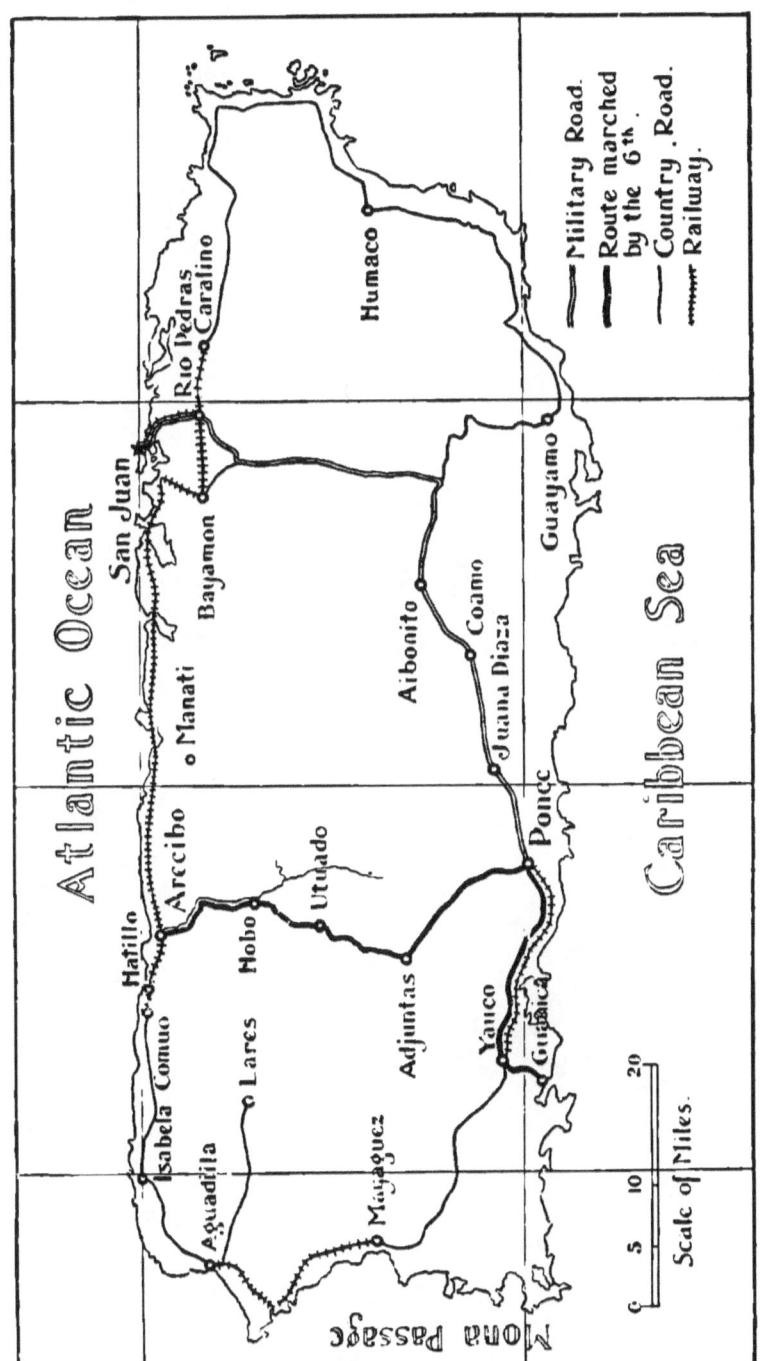

MAP OF PORTO RICO.

north of Guanica, from which point he was to go to Arecibo and there join General Henry's brigade in its advance on San Juan, either by rail or road. General Ernst with another division marched out over the military road direct from Ponce towards Aibonito ; while General Garretson's brigade, which

ROAD FROM PONCE TO HARBOR.

included the 6th Massachusetts, left Ponce on the 9th of August, marching directly north towards Arecibo over a mountain trail that was considered impassable for anything but a native pony, and through a section of country where we were told the English language had never been heard.

The march northward across the island was started Tuesday morning at 8.30, August 9, with the 2d battalion of the 6th, under Major Priest, as advance guard.

The plaza in Ponce had been left three hours behind when the regiment was overtaken on the road by the new commander, Col. Edmund Rice, accompanied by Captain Edgerton of West Point and J. N. Taylor, correspondent of the "Globe." Marching had just been resumed after a rest, when the new commander rode up, having made rather slow progress after overtaking the bull train about four miles out of Ponce.

The colonel was introduced by Captain Edgerton, who returned to Ponce soon after. The colonel rode ahead, overtaking General Henry at the point near the first camp where the good road merges into the bad. A mile from this point is a little settlement called Guaraguaves, at the summit of a long hill, but nestled away itself in the pocket formed by hills rising almost perpendicularly for five hundred to two thousand five hundred feet. There was no level ground for camp, so the men took to the slopes on the side of a hill which was so steep that braces were built to keep them from slipping down during the night. To lie on the poncho was equal to sleeping on a toboggan slide, and in the morning the men found that they

Colonel Edmund Rice.

and their belongings had parted company by many yards.

It was here that during the night the 6th Illinois regiment, camped near us, was stampeded by the bulls running down the hill through their camp at night, injuring several of them.

Colonel Rice and Lieutenant Colonel Ames took the oath binding them to duty as colonel and lieutenant colonel of the 6th about nine o'clock Tuesday evening. The following morning our

A NATIVE EXPRESS.

officers were ready for a prompt start, but it was nearly noon when the 6th Illinois took the lead.

August 10. From this point the road ceased to be a road, and we entered on the trail which General Stone had undertaken to make passable for the troops. To accomplish this a thousand natives had been put to work, who greeted us with cheers and the conventional " Mericano mucho bueno " as they stood aside for the troops to pass. Their superintendents each carried an ugly-looking whip, which they did not hesitate to use on their employees if there was occasion. It was afterwards reported that many of the best men had been transferred

"Dutch Yoke."

from the work on the pass, and that the government had paid them for working on the plantations of the superintendents.

The day's march took the regiment to the plantation of Pouvenir, after having marched the entire afternoon through a pouring rain, and ended the day by fording greatly swollen streams. As an attack was considered possible at any time, the men had been sent in light marching order, their rolls being carried by the ox teams in the rear of the column.

The wagons went heavily loaded, and as the regiment did not have its full quota of these, it was necessary to economize weight. That Captain Ham was conscientious in the discharge of his

"A Porto Rican Picnic."

duties, no one will doubt, and he will be remembered unto the third and fourth generation. One day a parrot which one of the men had carried many days was allowed to perch on top of one of the wagons, until the Captain espied it, when, as there could be no extra weight carried, he told the parrot to get off its perch. The parrot said, "Get to ——!" then, as if having forgotten it was not speaking to a private, began speaking so rapidly in Spanish it was impossible to follow it.

When night fell, the men were camped without cover or protection of any kind at the plantation, the teams containing rolls and all provisions being far in the rear and unable, owing to the bad condition of the roads, to reach the camp that night. Different companies managed to start fires about which they spent the night, where at eleven o'clock volunteers who had returned for coffee arrived with a sufficient quantity to give the respective companies that comfort, which was their only supper.

This was without exception the worst night spent by the regiment during the summer. About midnight a coal-bin under headquarters was discovered, which had been overlooked by the men in their search for shelter. Four soldiers, three of whom were Harvard men, crawled into the charcoal and there spent the night, which one of them described as being comparatively the most comfortable night he had ever spent, the charcoal absorbing the water from their clothing and enabling them to lie down.

If the college men, of whom we had an unusually large proportion, lacked the muscle with which their stronger brothers were blessed, they made up for it in determination and grit. Of this march, Roy Martin wrote: —

"There is not a general who will not say a good word about the dude soldiers. Gentlemen cannot afford to do their work poorly. One day, after a hard day's march beyond Adjuntas, when the men were hungry, tired, and soaked to the skin, a major asked for volunteers to go back after enough food to refresh the men. This was in a regiment not known as a dude regiment. Five men volunteered, and a weary set of men they were, too. Four of them were graduates of Harvard and the other was a graduate of Technology. They were dudes. Whenever hereafter I hear a Socialist on Boston Common damning all wealthy persons, I shall feel like asking him what he was doing while so many of the American dudes were cleaning the guns, watering the mules, and eating hardtack in Porto Rico.

"The spirit of such soldiers is inspiring. They neither boast of themselves nor underrate their enemies, but I never doubted for an instant that if General Wilson ordered the men to charge on Aibonito Pass, as it was expected he would, not a dude soldier would have flinched, though death would have claimed all who went first. I never doubted, either, that if he had called for volunteers every one would have instantly reported himself as ready and anxious for the opportunity to do or die."

One company had been fortunate enough to find shelter under an old shed, where during the night a big tarantula crawled across a man's face and wakened him. He screamed and started to run, awakening the others who were near him. They all ran out of the shed, crawling over the men outside, and started a stampede which did not end short of the river, twenty feet below, when the men became sufficiently awakened to realize it was not a Spaniard.

A large pigeon-cote was the only visible market, and this was patronized so constantly during the night that nothing but patches of feathers about the ground the following morning told of a " cote to let."

During the night the horse of one of the officers fell over the embankment in the rear of headquarters and broke his neck.

August 11. The following morning the regiment pushed on to the top of the divide over a road of wet clay, reaching the summit of the mountain, from which the harbor of Ponce was plainly visible, and from a point a short distance beyond, the sea on the north side of the island could be seen, the day's march ending at Adjuntas at 3 P. M., where another terrible night was spent in mud and rain.

August 12. The regiment remained in camp at Adjuntas, with heavy rains all day. Rumors of the enemy's depredations, most of them false or misleading, were being received every hour. Peace rumors were also in circulation, and there was much restlessness under the restraint of slow marching. Late Thursday afternoon, August 12, reports of General Schwan's engagement with the enemy near Hormigueros the day before reached camp, making everybody wish for an advance. Late that evening, when eight companies of the 6th Massachusetts were ordered forward, there were pleasant anticipations as to what the morrow might bring forth.

August 13. Dawn was greeted by reveille, and before eight o'clock, Colonel Rice had left with Companies A, H, G, and C of Captain Gihon's battalion and I, D, L, and M of Major Priest's command. Three days' rations and one hundred rounds of ammunition were given each man, while a mule pack-train with five days' rations and extra ammunition followed. Major Darling's battalion and the whole of the 6th Illinois regiment was left in Adjuntas to guard the town and bring up supplies. There was no delay on this march, as the men expected to see Spaniards. Four companies of the 19th were to be picked up at Utuado, and Arecibo would have been made in another day.

The march to Utuado, of eighteen miles, which had been considered a two days' journey, was made without great exertion in one day, when Gen. Guy N. Henry said to the men of the 6th and Colonel Rice: "You are doing splendidly; not a man has straggled unless he was actually prostrated by the sun — ten times as many men of the 6th Illinois have fallen out."

From Adjuntas to Utuado he said to Colonel Rice, "Take it easy and stop half way for the night." The regiment went through in one day, and on arrival at Utuado he said, "Boys, you did better than the regulars."

On our arrival we were told of the signing of the protocol, and instead of pushing on toward Arecibo, as was expected, we were to go into camp indefinitely. We marched by the town underneath the walls of the village cemetery, which were punctured by portholes made by the Spanish soldiers for our reception, and camped in an old sugar-cane field on the banks of a river, which in another season of the year would have been an excellent location. But it was the beginning of the rainy season, and the first downpour turned the camp into a mire. Day after day the rains continued until the ground, which absorbed water like a sponge, was thoroughly saturated. When the sun shone, as it did a part of each day, it was only to cause a vapor to rise from the mire and hasten the decay of the rank vegetation which had been trampled into the mud. Drains were dug which did not drain but which increased the foul odors from freshly-turned soil. On every opportunity all articles of clothing and blankets would be exposed to the sun, only to be

Utuado

saturated again with rain before night. There was no flooring for the tents, the men being obliged to sleep for nearly two weeks on this wet ground with nothing but their blankets for protection, until the increasing length of the line which answered sick call each morning warned officials that a change must be made. For the first time since leaving Camp Alger the spirits of the men were broken. Singing and all forms of camp amusements which furnished their daily entertainment were broken off, and when night fell, a gloom and stillness pervaded the camp that meant despair in the hearts of the men. The bugle calls could no longer sound the challenge either of "Good boy, Donivan" or the equally familiar invitation to "Go out in the woods," the absence of which calls was more significant of the state of mind of the men than could be told in volumes.

Food was scarce, and what there was had to be cooked in the insufficient utensils it had been possible to carry, without cover of any kind for a cook house. As it rained invariably at meal time there were no complaints of the soup or the coffee being too strong.

August 15. The band, two ambulances, and some pack-mules arrived from Adjuntas, and outposts were established about four miles out on the Arecibo road. The band was quartered in a shed where they were able to continue practice regardless of the rain.

August 16. Major Darling with Companies E. K. and B arrived from Adjuntas, together with the 6th Illinois. Company F being left there on provost duty until the 20th.

August 17. Continuous rain during the past two days. An outpost was established on the Lares road, the 6th Illinois alternating with our regiment.

As there seemed to be no immediate prospect of getting on to Arecibo or receiving supplies from that direction, seventy bull-teams were sent back to Ponce for supplies.

The noise attendant on the arrival of such a train is peculiar to nothing else. The creaking of the heavy, clumsy, overloaded carts, the nasal tones of the excited drivers yelling "Weis," and other like words, the prodding of the tired animals, created an excitement equal to the arrival of a circus in a country town.

Mr. Dwight L. Rogers wrote from Utuado, August 20th: —

"This place is in a valley among the hills. Our camp is situated on what we are told is the River of Life, a stream which at this season runs torpid and swollen with the rains. We hope we shall not have to stay long on this ground, as the mud is terrible.

Thus far I have kept fairly dry, except my feet, which are soaked all the time. Some of the men tell me they have not been dry, day or night, for over a week. Thus far, however, they seem to be standing the exposure well. I am still messing with Company I, and find the Concord boys a fine lot of fellows. Our soldiers were glad to enlist, and as long as there is need they are willing to do their duty, but if the war is over they are exceedingly anxious to go home.

"The boys, as I have said, appreciate any little thing the Association can do for them. Hardly a day passes but what some of the Fitchburg boys tell what a great send-off the Y. M. C. A. gave them when they came away from there, and others I often hear say, 'I am going to join the Association as soon as I get back.' The boys who left school are now anxious to be back in time to start the year with their classes."

On Sunday service was to have been held as usual by Mr. Rogers at ten o'clock, but, owing to a misunderstanding with the band and their not arriving at that hour, it was postponed until four o'clock. The colonel, being engaged and not knowing of the postponement, walked out in front of his tent and saw what he supposed to be the "congregation" assembled at one corner of the camp. He was not aware of the presence of two "mascots" in the form of fighting pups, or of the tendency of these animals to meet on Sunday.

"Orderly," he called to the young man outside his tent. "Yes, sir," replied the orderly, saluting.

"Is that the church service taking place over there?" "No, sir; that is a dog fight," replied the orderly, saluting again. The shock to the colonel was only apparent to those who saw him when he quietly turned and walked into Major Darling's tent, where he sat on a cot and laughed

NATIVES BATHING AT "MUD HOLE."

until the perspiration ran down his sun-burned face in drops as large as coffee berries.

One comfort we did have, and that was good bathing facilities. If we got baths unexpectedly and without our consent occasionally, it was made up for by the comfort of having a bath each day. Without exception each camp the regiment had in Porto Rico was near water where we were not only able to have a daily bath but to wash our clothing

UTUADO.

as well. Some idea of the heat of the sun may be gained from this. The men would wash their canvas suits, leggings, etc., and spread them on the rocks to dry while they took a plunge. At the end of fifteen or twenty minutes everything would be perfectly dry and warm. Thanks to the laundry facilities, the danger of clothing becoming inhabited was almost entirely averted, the exceptional cases being usually due to the neglect of the individual.

August 22. Colonel Rice left for Ponce with his orderly to obtain permission to move the men into barracks in town, as there seemed to be no immediate prospect of our moving on to Arecibo.

August 24. Company E was detailed for provost duty in town. The same day a telegram arrived from Colonel Rice ordering the regiment to break camp and go into town, occupying in part the quarters vacated by the four companies of the 19th infantry, who with General Henry and staff had left for Ponce.

Coffee warehouses and one school-house were called into requisition, which gave the men dry quarters and good cooking houses, even if they were crowded and the buildings were infested with the ubiquitous flea. While supplies were still limited in quantity and variety, as they had to be brought by pack-mules over the mountain trail from Ponce, there was a decided improvement in rations which was helped out by the local market, although the scarcity of money in the regiment made this of comparatively small benefit.

Lieutenant Hart left on the 23d, called home by sickness in his family.

UTUADO, August 24, 1898.

The greatest enemy the boys have had to deal with is mud, and in some of the roads it was anywhere from one to ten inches deep, with the sticking tendency greater than any found in old Virginia.

Perhaps you have read about how we lost our colonel, lieutenant colonel, major, chaplain, and a few other officers of the regiment. There is not one of us that knows the true reason of their retirement, but there are lots of rumors in the air about it. Well, we have a regular army officer as our colonel now, and best of all, he is a Massachusetts man. Since he took charge of the regiment we have fared a good deal better than we have since we enlisted. In anything that pertains to our duty he is very strict, but when off duty we can enjoy ourselves to the best of our ability.

There are so many sick on account of our last camp that we have been moved into barracks, an old unoccupied storehouse in nice condition, with plenty of air, whitewashed, and with hard cement floors which we call our bed. Night before last I hung up a hammock made by tying up the ends of my half of the tent. As true as I am here I could not sleep, being used to hard surfaces. Finally I gave it up and went on to the floor, where I slept as sound as a log.

This morning, which is a good example of our daily

Utuado

routine, was spent as follows: Roll call 5.15, breakfast 5.30 to 6.30, consisting of bean soup, one half cup to a man, with five hardtacks. The boys have offered a reward to the one finding a bean in his soup. This is followed by one drill in the morning that lasts about one hour. Dinner at 12 noon, which consists of one half cup of rice, a little sugar, and five tacks. One drill in the afternoon lasting one hour. Retreat, lowering

THE SOLDIERS' CEMETERY, UTUADO.

the colors, and roll call at 5.15. Supper at six consists of one piece of bacon, five tacks, and one cup of coffee.

Five funerals of the natives have passed our barracks to-day, and an odd sight they were, too. They have no procession except when a wealthy person dies; then there is a very small one. The only procession the common folks have is the pall bearers. The coffin, or rather box, is strapped with two long pieces of bamboo, and is carried on the shoulders of the pall bearers, and has no lid. When they reach the cemetery they take the corpse out of the coffin and place it in a small tomb, put a shovel of earth on it, and let it remain there until the worms eat the flesh from the bones; then they take the bones out and pile them up in the corner and put another body in the hole. The wealthier class have a common black coffin like ours and are buried in it and never removed. I saw three corpses yesterday of victims of starvation. They were children of about five to ten years of age and their throats were very little bigger than my two fingers. It was a frightful sight. The cemetery here has a high thick wall around it, and the Spaniards have cut little portholes in it and use them as a sort of breastwork or fort.[1]

August 28. Dr. Washburn, Lieutenant Sweetser, and J. N. Taylor of the " Globe " went through to Arecibo under the protection of a pillow case, which was adapted for a white flag, and got permission to transport hospital supplies through the city which had been sent from Ponce on the "Alamo." The commandante was most courteous in his reception of the detail and had a squad of his own men assist in starting the stores on the way to Utuado, including stores and clothing sent by Colonel Rice from Ponce.

The 6th Illinois with General Garretson and staff left at 8 A.M. for the States to be mustered out. A gloom was cast over the camp by the sad death of one of the 6th Illinois men in the hospital,

[1] Quoted from a letter of a member of Company B.

FREDERIC A. WASHBURN,
First Lieutenant and Assistant Surgeon.

supposed to be due to melancholia at being left behind by his regiment.

August 31. This was a red-letter day, as mail arrived from home, and the clothing for the men came as a result of one of the first orders given by Colonel Rice to have the entire regiment fitted out with new uniforms, shoes, and hats, as the men were fast reaching the condition of Gunga Din. when —

> "The uniform he wore,
> Was nothing much before
> An' rather less than 'arf o' that be'ind."

They had become literally "hobos" in appearance and were so entirely uncomfortable when the new suits arrived that no one would venture out so "dressed up" until the regiment was ordered to appear for parade.

Extract from a private's diary.

Monday — Breakfast, tomato soup, hardtack, and coffee; dinner and supper, the same.

Tuesday — For each meal, two hardtack, tomato soup, small piece of bread.

Wednesday — For breakfast and dinner, tomato soup, coffee, two hardtack, and bread; for supper the following extras were served: two small pieces of corn bread, two inches square, with some sirup, one spoonful of scrambled eggs, half water, one handful of oyster crackers, tomato soup, and coffee.

Thursday and Friday — Tomato soup, hardtack, and coffee again, with a little corn bread on Friday.

Sept. 1. Private A. S. Cushman of Company A, who was in charge of the pioneer corps, received a commission as captain of subsistence and left at once for the States by way of Ponce.

Sept. 2. The quartermaster issued the much needed clothing to the men.

No history of the regiment in Porto Rico would be complete were the name of Mrs. Rice, the wife of the colonel, omitted. On the 2d of September, Colonel Rice arrived from Ponce, accompanied by Mrs. Rice, having crossed the trail so recently considered impassable in General Miles's carriage, Mrs. Rice being the first English woman, so far as known, to have been in that part of the island.

The day after her arrival she visited the hospital, and from that time until her departure, her entire strength and energies were given to our sick men. All the attentions possible in the power of one woman, of personal exertion and suggestion combined, were given to the hospitals. She remained in Utuado until the regiment left for Arecibo, where she went together with Miss Galt and Miss Parsons, being obliged to make the journey over the mountain trail in the saddle owing to the rivers being impassable.

Mrs. Colonel Rice.

Utuado

Her self-sacrificing devotion to the welfare of the men has endeared her name to every man who knew her in the hospitals, and has given to all a memory and respect of an American woman the

HEAVY MARCHING ORDER INSPECTION.

mention of whose name is the signal for the doffing of the regimental hat.

Occasional miscalculations were made in the judgment of officials, as when, one of the wagon wheels having broken down going over the mountain, Lieutenant ―――― said he could duplicate it easily, as there was another wagon of the same make in camp. As the roads were in a terrible condition and there were no available teams by which to send the wheel out, the colonel told two of the prisoners proper allowance would be made in their punishment, if they wished to roll the wheel out and substitute it for the broken one. They gladly undertook the mission, and they earned all they got in rebate, for the roads were deep with mud and it was up the mountains most of the way. After hours of weary climbing the prisoners arrived totally exhausted with the wheel, and found that, while the wheel was the same make, Lieutenant ———, like the tailor who cut off the wrong leg of the trousers for the one-legged man, had sent the front wheel instead of the hind one.

Lieut. Thomas Talbot arrived from Ponce, having been to Cuba and returned to the United States in trying to reach the regiment. On arrival he was assigned to Company M, being later transferred to Company E.

September 5. First Lieut. Clarence W. Coolidge of Company E was appointed adjutant, *vice* Lieut. F. E. Gray, while owing to the absence of Lieutenant Hart, Lieut. George W. Braxton of Company L was appointed acting ordnance officer.

UTUADO, Sept. 6, 1898.

How about our own regiment? The spirits of the men have improved a little since they have gotten under cover, but this is not child's play here. Night after night there are men going to sleep hungry. United States soldiers going to sleep hungry! It is a sad thought. Do the officials deny it? If they do, they misrepresent the facts. Quantity and quality of food are both plain. The officers often fail to realize what differences there are between the fare of the enlisted men and what they have. I have messed with both a great deal, and I have never yet found an officer's mess without a number of delicacies privates lack. If the men had a little spending money to get a pineapple or an orange or a piece of bread now and then, it would make eating less mechanical.

"The troops have been paid promptly," says Washington. Perhaps those at home have. But not a cent has been paid to a volunteer in Porto Rico. I have taken the pains to find the truth in this matter. If there has been a paymaster on this island he has not presented himself at headquarters yet. Is Porto Rico on the maps at Washington? "There is too much criticism of the War Department," says the reader, perhaps. But when men give up business and home and everything else to do soldier's duty in August in the tropics, they ought to have hundreds of things our soldiers lack. Where are the thin clothes? Where are the shoes? Where are the sheets for the hospitals? Where are the postmasters? Where are the nurses? Where are the indications that somebody realizes the dangers of this climate and the hardships of a soldier's life?

I am afraid if the 6th Massachusetts should march up Beacon Hill to-day those who looked at the faces of these men would be shocked. The tan does not obscure the traces of rough usage. The look of patience does not obliterate the marks of hardship.

"It will be different when we get to Arecibo," runs the general current of camp talk.

FREDERICK ROY MARTIN.

Twice a day the companies were drilled, and a range of two hundred yards having been established, squads were taken out regularly to practise with the new rifle. The days after drill were spent almost entirely in quarters. Even the men who were considered well had lost all superfluous energy and strength, and were glad to be quiet when possible. Magazines and papers were once more arriving and were eagerly welcomed by the men. The stillness of the hot hours of the day was broken only by the little natives whirling carelessly the well-balanced boxes of candy on their heads, and singing their " Dulce Mericano " in a musical voice, which you soon learned as they grew older would take the sharp nasal twang of their parents.

Early morning would find a number of men patrolling the market-place ready to seize a stray egg at " Cinco centavos," as one or two materialized from the mosaic of vegetables done up in a native's handkerchief, or with a tin cup waiting for the cow to be driven in to buy their pint of milk. These were luxuries, however, which few could afford until after the paymaster arrived the third of October.

The band, which had literally " played out " on the marches with the other men, immediately on its arrival at Utuado, when it was fortunate enough to be under cover in a sugar-house, began systematic practice, with the most gratifying results. The improvement was remarked by every one, and by the time the regiment had recuperated sufficiently to have parade in town, the

UTUADO MARKET SCENE.

band played with a brilliancy we had not before heard.

The bugle corps were called into service, and were truly a credit to themselves and the regiment.

When the band gave an evening concert in the Plaza, the entire population would congregate there, and furnish such contrasts as can only be described by children dressed "only in a smile" promenading between the young society girls, who in their bright colored and smart city gowns, under the glare of the up-to-date electric lights, were quite willing to be admired and to show their degree of civilization in their liking for uniforms.

September 8. Last night a member of Company I had a nightmare and gave vent to the most

GOING TO THE CONCERT.

frightful yell ever heard, so that the men sleeping near him were sure the "Black Hand" were murdering some one of them, when they yelled and started a stampede, which ended outside the building.

Lieutenant La Croix arrived last night from

Ponce with teams bringing the rifles, ammunition, and other supplies which had been left behind.

September 10. Regimental inspection was held at 9 A. M. by Colonel Rice.

September 11. Major Darling arrived with ten teams, bringing clothing and medical supplies from Ponce.

The game of leap frog, which the men used to play evenings, or for exercise in the mornings, afforded the natives great amusement, and introduced a new sport to the boys.

After nearly two months the 6th had been held in Utuado, while the Spanish occupied Arecibo, and although many interchanges of courtesies had taken place and the Spanish commandante had shown himself most accommodating in the matter of permitting the passage of hospital supplies and sick through his lines, it was not until well along in September that rations and other necessities had come in other than by the long, hard road to Ponce, often impassable by reason of heavy landslides.

September 15. Mail arrived at noon, and evening parade was reviewed by Colonel Rice in front of the church.

A telegram was received by the colonel from General Henry, commanding at Ponce: "Have five companies prepared to move to places to be vacated by Spanish troops in the northwestern part of Porto Rico. Places to which they will have to go and time they will have to reach them will be communicated later."

The "Bay State" arrived in Ponce on the 14th, and on the 16th Dr. Crockett rode into camp on a cavalry horse loaned by General Henry. There was much speculation about the home trip of the sick, as one hundred was the limit of the ship's capacity, but twice that number were unfit for duty and anxious to go. Dr. Burrell, after learning of the condition of the roads, decided to sail around to Arecibo, in which port the "Bay State" anchored late on the afternoon of the 19th. At seven the next morning eighteen wagons loaded with sick were started for Arecibo, with Dr. Crockett in charge, arriving without incident, and on the morning of the 22d the ship sailed for Boston.

September 18. The improved condition of the regiment was noticeable in its entire life to its own members, and that it was so to others is testified by the following words from a member of the staff of General Brooke : —

"The neatness of the men on duty, evidence of military system, good behavior of the men on the street, and tone of the command is like that of a regiment of regulars, and there exists an *esprit* among the officers and men and a devotion to the colonel which I have not seen in other volunteer commands."

On the 18th Lieutenant Colonel Ames was placed in charge of civil affairs, and Company C of the 6th was sent to Lares to relieve the Spanish garrison and guard plantations thereabouts. Details of from two to ten men were guarding property for thirty miles around.

September 19. One company of the 1st Kentucky (mounted) had been added to the Utuado garrison, ninety-two sturdy-looking soldiers from the blue-grass State having ridden in to report for duty to Colonel Rice. Reports of depredations by the "Black Hand," an organization of desperadoes and robbers, were coming with telegraphic rapidity. The jail in Utuado was full of offenders, but that kind of punishment had no terrors for them.

September 22. Considering the opportunities offered by a misunderstanding of our language, casualties were rare. One native failing to answer the third or fourth challenge given by the guard on the plantation of Antonio Marques was shot and killed by a member of the 6th. No possible blame can be attached to the soldier, as he did strictly and only his duty.

Company K on the 28th relieved Company E of provost duty, who had since the leaving of the regulars had that work. On the same day Company I started for Coamo, followed on the 6th of October by Company E for Hatillo.

As each company left town they were escorted by the band out over the bridge by the old camp and given a " God speed " by the colonel.

On the 30th of September the members of Company I were very greatly surprised to see the Rev. Mr. McDonald of Concord walking down the streets of Utuado. He had come in behalf of the families of the men in the company, and particularly for the purpose of taking home the bodies of those who had died there.

Only those personally familiar with the country, and the difficulty of travelling, can know what it meant to undertake the office of kindness which Mr. McDonald accomplished. His visit to the regiment cheered up all the men, and his sermon on Sunday, October 2, on the importance of the service of those who " only stand and wait " was at a time when men were forgetting the life of the soldier is spent principally in service of waiting, but always ready.

The following interesting letter was written by Mr. McDonald shortly after his arrival at Utuado.

" The journey from Ponce to this place is extremely interesting. I started Wednesday morning with five doctors in a mule wagon. The first ten miles the road was fair. Then it became so bad that the wagon got stalled in the middle of a river ford. From there I walked ten miles with one of the doctors to a town called Adjuntas, where I stayed over night. The next morning I succeeded in finding a mule and afterward a saddle. The animal at first seriously objected to my weight on his back, but after a struggle, in which I finally brought up in an orange grove, the mule discovered what a masterly hand held the bridle, and started on the way without further protest. I was on his back for about four hours, which brought me to Utuado.

"The whole journey from Ponce to Utuado is through the most magnificent scenery. At times the road or path was on the edge of a precipice nearly two thousand feet deep, and sometimes if the mule had made a misstep, I should not be here to write this letter. Mountain heights and deep ravines are filled with a luxuriant foliage, with orange, banana, coffee trees, and sugar cane. The natives picked me a bunch of oranges and bananas for a penny. The whole ride was immensely enjoyable.

"One of the first men to meet me in Utuado was Sergt. George King, and a more astonished and delighted boy you never saw. That night we had a reception in his quarters, and the talk was long and interesting. Among the boys I found Sergt. James Tolman very ill. He is now much better, and the doctor says that he considers him entirely out of danger. The boys now in the hospital whom you know are Bugler Philip Emmott and Robert Richardson. Bert Dakin is around, but looking miserable. Out of a thousand men the regiment has about three hundred and seventy sick, and very few of those who are not sick are really strong and well. It is the sickest place that I was ever in, and the whole business of this encampment seems to be to take care of the ailing. The boys have lost all the spare flesh they had, and we have some cases of living skeletons. I go through the three hospitals every day, saying a cheering word to every man, and it does me good to see their faces brighten up at the mention of home and the prospect of soon getting there.

"This afternoon I held a religious service in the square, and about five hundred of the well soldiers were present, and they seemed much helped by my words of comfort and cheer. The desire to go home is universal, and the intense longing on the part of some produces a sort of melancholia. I don't know why it is, whether it is the heat, or the unsatisfactory sanitary conditions of

SUNDAY IN UTUADO.

the place, or the miserable rations, but it certainly seems that if the men remain here two months longer there will not be a well man in the whole regiment.

"It is announced that a part of the regiment at least will be removed to Arecibo, on the coast, with much more healthful conditions. I have taken two or three detachments of our men to the hotel and given them one good square meal, the best that the town could furnish.

It was the first that some of them had had since starting from home, and was immensely appreciated. I was disappointed to find that some of our men, with Captain Cook, had been sent to a distant place the day before my arrival. I start on a journey of about thirty miles to-morrow to see them, expecting to return to Utuado again in a few days. I go on a horse furnished by Colonel Rice, who has been very kind to me since my arrival."

October 1. Regimental line inspection was held at 7.45 A. M. in heavy marching order, with shelter tents, rolls, haversacks, and canteens. In the afternoon the wagon train left in charge of Lieutenant Conrad for Arecibo for supplies.

October 3. Two ambulances and four teams left Utuado at 6 A. M. in charge of Surgeon Washburn with forty sick men for Arecibo, who were to return home on the hospital ship "Relief."

There had been numerous rumors of the coming of the paymaster, until the men had grown sceptical on the subject. When in the evening an ambulance drove into town with the paymaster in person, a welcome was accorded him which few officials received. Two hours later the detail which had gone to Arecibo on the 2d in charge of Sergeant Draper arrived with the paymaster's boxes.

October 4. A hospital train carrying twenty-nine men for the "Relief" left Utuado at 7 A. M. The excitement attendant on the arrival of the paymaster the night before pervaded the regiment during the morning. At 12.30 Major Doyon began paying the men, finishing that evening. As the companies lined up with a number in the ranks that had not been seen there for many days, there was much friendly chaffing as to the increase among the different companies, over the "lame and the halt," who with difficulty stood in line

A NATIVE PACK TRAIN.

until, as they say in the navy, the circle had been made the second time, and the men had the first money they had received in three months. If some of them forgot they were "sick in quarters" they are not to be blamed.

Before the line was half passed men were hurrying to the different stores in the town to get change in Porto Rican money. A harvest such as the town had never before seen was garnered by the shopkeepers, many of whom to their lasting shame raised prices until they had to be threatened with having their shops closed.

The hotels and restaurants, such as they are, were taken by storm, until it was not possible to get a place for any price. Many men got the first "square meal" they had had since leaving Camp Alger in July. The colonel showed his confidence in the men by having taps an hour later in honor of the event, a privilege which was continued until the regiment left the town. That the men appreciated this was shown by the temperate use they made of their freedom and money, there being few cases of drunkenness or disorder in the town. After the needs of clothing, etc., were supplied, the men began buying souvenirs, etc.

An event which would have been of great interest to the regiment any time but "pay day" was the raising of the American flag in Utuado, when Major Darling responded to the alcalde's address. As it was, there were more than thirteen stars visible that night, and the happiest crowd of men since leaving Camp Alger.

Rev. George D. Rice was commissioned chaplain of the 6th Massachusetts, filling the vacancy made by the resignation of Rev. Mr. Dusseault at Ponce. The return of the regiment shortly after this prevented the new chaplain from joining it until its return to Massachusetts.

Chaplain Rice was born in Malden in 1861, educated at the Mt. Vernon Military Academy, Chicago, and at Tufts College Divinity School.

On the breaking out of the war he was a member of Battery K, 1st Massachusetts Heavy Artillery.

October 5. Inspection of quarters and the personal appearance of the men was held at 5 P. M., and in the evening two pack trains arrived from Arecibo.

October 6. Company E, commanded by Lieutenant Moore, left for Isabella at 7.30 A. M., the band escorting them out of the town, where they were reviewed by Colonel and Mrs. Rice at the bridge.

Before they had proceeded far a messenger overtook them to tell of the arrival of the telegram to Colonel Rice: " 6th Massachusetts Regiment to be ordered to United States. Regiment to remain until relieved."

This was the culmination of the efforts made when matters were at their worst for the regiment to be relieved and returned home.

The possibility of being able to report abuses and of their being righted in time was the only consolation for the men. Earlier letters detailing the story of the life of unnecessary hardships in a land of plenty and a period of practical peace

CHAPLAIN GEORGE D. RICE.

had been sent broadcast by the men to their homes; the results of which were mass meetings held in different towns and appeals to the governor for the return of the regiment that stimulated him to write the following kindly letter to President McKinley: —

Boston, Sept. 5, 1898.

To the President, Washington, D. C.

The pitiable condition in which the 2d and 9th Massachusetts regiments have returned from their arduous and gallant service in Cuba has naturally caused a profound sense of solicitude regarding the 6th regiment, now in Porto Rico. My own feelings are deeply concerned, and I am besought by personal letters and by the authorities of cities to ask for the prompt return and muster out of this regiment. I have felt it my duty to decline to comply with this request so long as the national government requires their services.

The splendid patriotism which prompted their voluntary enlistment will sustain them in any perils or hardships they may be called on to endure. But the lives of her sons are precious in the eyes of the commonwealth, as I am well assured they are to you, to whom the fortunes of our arms have been competently intrusted, and I have the honor urgently to request that whether in camp, in garrison, or on transports, these lives may be tenderly guarded by every precaution in clothing, food, and medical attendance which science may suggest.

To this end no effort can be too great and no expenditure too lavish. The commonwealth, through its constituted authorities, and through the contributions of its patriotic citizens, ably administered by the Voluntary

Aid Association, will consider it a privilege to be permitted, with money or supplies, to aid the efforts which the national government is making to render its service less perilous to the lives and health of its gallant soldiers. ROGER WOLCOTT.

By the time the machinery which granted this request was set in motion, the evils had been

STARTING FOR OUTPOST DUTY.

largely overcome and the health and spirits of the regiment were on the mend. The majority of the officers and many of the men preferred spending the winter in Porto Rico, and enjoying the life that had come to be pleasant after so long a period of preparatory work. The morning of October 6, during guard mount, Colonel Rice received telegraphic orders to move to Arecibo. His appreciation of the men's feeling was shown by his relieving the band from guard mount and

GOVENOR WOLCOTT.

sending them as a herald through the streets with the welcome news. An impromptu procession was formed behind the band, and the demonstration which took place left no room for doubts as to the opinion of the regiment on the subject.

October 9. Company B, commanded by Lieut.

NATIVE WATER CARRIER.

F. G. Taylor, left Utuado at 9.30 A. M. for Hatillo, going by way of Arecibo.

The prospect of going home gave life a new interest, and the "Bay State walk" was replaced by an elastic step that no other tonic could have effected in the same space of time.

October 10. The order was given for Companies I, H, K, and L to leave Utuado for Arecibo with Major Darling in command.

CHAPTER VIII

THE HOSPITALS

" What ha' you done with half your mess, Johnnie, Johnnie?
They could n't do more, and they would n't do less,
Johnnie, my Johnnie aha!
They ate their whack and they drank their fill,
And I think the rations has made them ill."

THE popular idea of an army hospital is one where rows of cots are filled by wounded heroes, minus arms, legs, etc., attended by an attractive trained nurse, immaculate in starched aprons and cuffs, with the badge of her office in the form of a red cross on her left arm. This idea, fostered by the newspaper, with a colored illustration showing a nurse at the bedside of an invalid propped up on big pillows, and with just a suggestion of romance thrown in, comes about as near the actuality of the early experiences of the 6th as the pretty milkmaid who appears in opera does to the real country maiden who fulfils that office on the farm. If mothers, whose chief care in the assistance of trained nurses at home consists in keeping folded screens properly placed to keep off drafts

MAJOR GEORGE F. DOW.
Surgeon.

and the shades drawn to a proper degree, could have seen their sons lying on the wet ground on only a blanket, or in a hospital wagon closed at *one* end during storms by a sheet, they would not have slept well.

Until the regiment went into quarters in Utuado we had the division hospital system. After that date, as our regiment was for the greater part of the time alone, the surgeons of the 6th had charge of their own men.

The first hospital opened in town, later known as No. 1, was in charge of Major Dow, Surgeons Washburn and Gross remaining with the regiment.

Previous to this time tents, later supplemented by the ambulances, had been used for hospital service, and as it was during the rainy season when we were located in the " mud hole " the transfer to the buildings of even warehouses was most acceptable. The simplicity of all houses on the island makes the difference between a house and a warehouse infinitely less than it would mean in this country.

Hospital No. 1 was a large coffee-house near the entrance to the village of Utuado as one arrives from Adjuntas or Arecibo. It was a long, narrow, one-story shed, raised on posts about six feet from the ground, sufficiently wide for two rows of cots, leaving a passage about four to five feet wide up and down the centre. This building was carefully cleaned, the walls were whitewashed, and put into a thoroughly good condition, accommodating about forty patients, leaving a comfortable interval between the cots. The patients nearly all had typhoid fever, and most of them at one time or another were very ill. An ell ran off from this coffee-shed in which were accommodated about ten more patients. In the yard of the coffee-house were pitched two hospital tents, containing each four cots for convalescent patients. Still back of this were pitched four common wall tents which were used by some of the hospital corps men and the cooks. On the same line with these tents were pitched two large flies for cook tents, one for cooking for the hospital corps men, and one for the patients. Still back of this another tent was pitched in which were kept supplies for the hospital, and yet further back was a long open shed in which slept the hospital corps men. Here they swung their hammocks, and had on the whole a very comfortable place in which to live. The sinks were well off to one side and back of the hospital, and were covered with earth three times a day, and large quantities of lime were used.

Hospital No. 2 was at the other end of the town, where were two coffee-houses with two yards between them used for the spreading of trays on which the coffee was dried. These coffee-houses were thoroughly cleaned and used in the same manner as described in Hospital No. 1. Hospital tents were pitched in the yards, and sinks were well in the rear. Hospital No. 2 was capable of holding from sixty to sixty-five patients.

Hospital No. 3 was a small house near the river, and accommodated from fifteen to twenty patients.

The first receipt of the much-needed delicacies and hospital supplies was from Arecibo, where Dr. Washburn went under the Red Cross flag, and from which place he was allowed to send medicinal supplies back to camp.

On first going into the hospitals there were almost no cots, and no bedding of any kind beyond the men's own blankets and ponchos. As fast as they could be made by the native carpenters, the native cots were manufactured and put into service. These consisted of canvas stretched on parallel bars, and were luxurious after a season on the ground and the floor.

There were a few cots in the town, but it was hard to find them. When one morning, therefore, Major ——— saw two men passing the hospital carrying a closed cot on their shoulders, he surprised them by rushing out and asking, "Quanto valé?—Quanto valé?" The natives looked surprised, and in their perplexity lowered the cot, when the doctor saw the corpse of a child in the folds of the canvas covering, which they were taking to the cemetery.

The absence of battles eliminated the care of wounded, but the rapidity with which the hospitals filled up gave the surgeons an equal amount of care. Fortune favored the regiment in not giving the combination.

Typhoid fever was the principal sickness, which at one time threatened to sweep the regiment, over half of it being "unfit for duty" at one time.

The danger of typhoid from the drinking water was always emphasized, and every pressure was brought to bear to have this boiled. During the marches it was impossible, and after going into quarters difficult. Under the direction of the medical staff a central boiling station was established, where boiled water was kept constantly on hand and supplied systematically to every company in the regiment. As a result of this, in a very short time there was a marked improvement in the health of the men.

The impression prevalent in this country that there was no typhoid in Porto Rico previous to the arrival of our troops is not accepted by our surgeons, who say there was plenty of it there on our arrival, and much more before the natives had time to contract it from the soldiers. Malaria also prevailed, but it was fortunately of a very mild type and yielded readily to treatment.

The need for nurses was imperative, as the large number of patients, most of whom were seriously ill at one time or another, requiring close attention, rendered the number of regular nurses entirely inadequate. Volunteers were called for, and men from the different companies volunteered with a cheerfulness that should be to their lasting credit, performing the arduous and continuous duties without complaint.

Kindness from a woman excites no comment. But when you see big strong men, clumsy though they be in their efforts, administering every possible attention to their sick comrades, it touches a chord that vibrates to no other experience.

The arrival of Mrs. Rice and later of Miss Galt and Miss Parsons brought into the hospitals the atmosphere and touch of comforts which usually are found in the wake of a woman in a sick-room.

Food for the hospitals was procured by sending men into the country for eggs and milk, while good bread was found in the local markets.

On September 23d the supplies sent by the Massachusetts Volunteer Aid Society on the " Bay State," consisting of cots, bedding, pajamas, linen, toilet articles, surgical appliances, drugs, rubber sheets, and fruit supplies were received. After this date the hospitals had everything wanted, and were able to distribute to the various companies a large stock of Red Cross supplies which were unsuitable for use in the hospitals.

For the men who were sick in quarters, that is, not ill enough to necessitate sending them to the

HOSPITAL LAUNDRY.

over-crowded hospital, a special diet was arranged at the hospital kitchens where the men went at stated hours.

The question of a laundry was a difficult problem to solve. At first the linen was sterilized as much as possible by wetting it down with solutions of antiseptics before being given to the native women for washing. Later two large iron kettles were set up in the rear of Hospital No.

Miss Muriel G. Galt.

3, where water was kept boiling constantly. Large coffee-sacks were distributed to each hospital, and as fast as the linen became soiled it was put directly into these and the sacks firmly tied. It was then taken to the kettles and boiled thoroughly before being removed, after which it was given to the Porto Rican women to wash.

The arrival of Miss Galt and Miss Parsons, who came down from the "Bay State" on her second trip, volunteering their services in the hospitals, was the greatest aid to the surgeons, Miss Parsons taking charge of Hospital No. 1, Miss Galt of No. 2, and between them looking after No. 3. Whatever feeling there may have been in the minds of a few of the men regarding the fitness of women nurses for an army hospital, was soon removed under the improved condition of affairs and the personal magnetism of the nurses.

One young man who was ill many weeks in the hospital writes: "Be sure and give the lady nurses, who were so kind to us who had to experience hospital life, all the credit due them. Most men are inclined to overlook the sacrifices made by these women when they are telling their own stories."

Typhoid being the principal disease, every possible precaution to prevent its spread was taken. Each nurse was given particular directions as to care of himself as well as his patient, and no convalescent from typhoid was allowed to return to his company for fear of possible infection.

The policy of the physicians was to send home only the men who were convalescent from typhoid, or those who were sick in quarters, being weak from exhaustion and unfit for service, and

Dr. Crockett.

who did not seem to be able to recuperate in that climate. The attitude assumed by the surgeons on this point is doubtless the reason the death rate among such a large number of typhoid patients was kept so small.

When able to be moved, they were transferred to Arecibo, where they were put aboard the hospital ships for home, the first detachment being sent on October the 3d and 4th by the "Relief," the rest of the men coming on the "Bay State."

On September 18th, Dr. Crockett arrived from Ponce, having made the trip in the saddle to see if it was feasible to transfer our sick men over that route to the "Bay State." As permission was gotten to send the sick men through by the way of Arecibo, the "Bay State" was sent to that point, where, on the 20th, seventy-eight of our men were sent in wagons under the care of Dr. Crockett. Some were so ill they were obliged to be transported in hammocks suspended in the wagons, but the journey was made without mishap.

The transfer to Arecibo was made in ambulances and army wagons drawn by four mules, over a road leading over mountains, around dangerous precipices where two wagons could not possibly pass, down slopes where the wagons jumped from one shelving rock to another, over roads that were cut into chuck holes where the wagon would plunge up to the bed in mud and water. The river, which had to be forded six times, was at this season very high from the heavy rains, and each trip that was made had to be prearranged and the chances taken of the river being reached after five hours' driving and found too deep to cross. As it was in many cases, the men had to stand up to keep out of the water, which would come up into the beds of the wagons, soaking everything that was left there.

On reaching Arecibo, there being no harbor there, it was necessary to transfer the sick into lighters, in which they were taken out to the hospital ship, which it was necessary to anchor far out from the shore. The excitement attendant on

HOSPITAL TRAIN FOR ARECIBO.

the departure of the sick for the hospital ships permeated the entire regiment. Nothing was harder for the sick in the hospital than to see others start home, while for the well men it was a temptation to want to be "just sick enough" to be candidates for the trip.

This work of transfer was done by army mules. Those who remember the struggle of the poor beasts as they plunged into the swift currents and struggled out over the muddy banks, who saw them day after day doing the work that horses could not possibly have done, and living on worse than army rations, will not underestimate the value of those animals in the Porto Rican campaign, or see inconsistency in remembering them kindly.

CONVALESCENTS ON THE WAY TO THE "BAY STATE."

A learned writer on the Holy Scriptures says: "It is acknowledged that neither the Apostles nor Fathers have absolutely condemned swearing, or the use of oaths, upon every occasion, and upon all subjects. There are circumstances wherein we cannot morally be excused from it; but we never ought to swear but upon urgent necessity, and to do some considerable good by it."

This may in a small degree apply to certain remarks made by our mule drivers before they learned to "speak Spanish" to the mules on the trips to Arecibo over the mountains.

The life of the surgeons in the midst of this amount of sickness, where disease had to be fought in the tropics with insufficient supplies and appliances, can only be imagined.

The day began with sick call at 7.30 A.M., when the sick men would line up by companies at the dispensary, being seen in turn by the surgeon and prescribed for, one being sent to the hospital, another returned to quarters, until the entire number had been seen, ranging from fifty to two hundred men who would have been in line.

From the dispensary, the surgeon would go to the hospitals, where he would join the others in the care of the patients there.

Under this strain Major Dow broke down and returned home on the "Bay State" from Arecibo on her second trip, presumably a sick man. When the boat returned the surprise of the regiment was only equalled by its delight at the return of Major Dow, who again took up his work until the return of the regiment.

The very small percentage of deaths out of the large number of cases of typhoid bears witness in a stronger way than anything that can be written of the care given our sick.

Stephen E. Ryder.   Edwin D. Towle.
Harrie C. Hunter.
Hospital Stewards.

Many severe criticisms have been made during the war of the treatment of certain regiments at the hands of their surgeons. The 6th has nothing but praise and an acknowledgment of their appreciation for the surgeons, who were untiring in their discharge of duty.

CHAPTER IX

THE "BAY STATE"

ON the third day of May, 1898, at the request of Governor Wolcott, a number of gentlemen whom he had asked as public-spirited citizens met in the council chamber to consider the advisability of the formation of a sanitary commission. As a result of this meeting, the Massachusetts Volunteer Aid Association was formed to render aid to the volunteers who enlisted in the service of the United States, with the following officers: —

EBEN S. DRAPER, *Chairman;* MAJOR H. L. HIGGINSON, *Treasurer;* ELIHU B. HAYES, *Secretary.*

Executive Committee.

HENRY L. HIGGINSON.	ARNOLD A. RAND.
GEORGE VON L. MEYER.	CHARLES J. PAINE.
EBEN S. DRAPER.	ROBERT M. BURNETT.
PATRICK A. COLLINS.	T. JEFFERSON COOLIDGE, JR.
ELIHU B. HAYES.	SHERMAN HOAR.
JAMES PHILLIPS, JR.	

At this meeting the suggestion was made by Dr. Herbert L. Burrell that a hospital ship would be of special use, and that a popular subscription should be started to buy and equip, under the Geneva conference, Article XIII, which is an international agreement, providing for the recognition of aid association ships, a volunteer Aid Association Ship. Our government hospital ships numbered but two; the "Relief" for the army and the "Solace" for the navy. The rapidity with which men broke down under tropical fevers rendered a greater transporting facility almost a necessity. The decision having been reached to purchase a ship, a public subscription was called for, to which the people of the State responded with a readiness and generosity that will be to the lasting glory of Massachusetts. The "widow's mite" and the five thousand dollar checks came together, $230,000 being promptly subscribed, and this amount could have been increased indefinitely. The question arising as to the function of the ship, whether it were to be primarily a supply one, not only for our troops but for combatants as well, or whether she were to be primarily a hospital ship, was settled by the consideration of Honorable Sherman Hoar, who came forward and solved the question by demonstrating to our government at Washington the necessity and the advisability of putting such a ship into commission.

During the month of May, R. M. Burnett, Esq.,

and Dr. C. A. Siegfried, after looking over various vessels which were offered, finally bought the "Bowden," one of the Boston Fruit Company's steamers, which arrived in Boston, June 6. She was sent to the Atlantic works of East Boston, where under the personal supervision of their consulting engineer, James T. Boyd, she was transformed and renamed the "Bay State," being the first aid association ship that had ever been fitted out under the Geneva conference, Article XIII.

This was done under the direction of the board of control, composed of Major Henry L. Higginson, Robert M. Burnett, Esq., and Dr. Herbert L. Burrell, with Dr. E. H. Bradford acting in the absence of Dr. Burrell, with James T. Boyd as consulting engineer. In seven weeks she was thoroughly renovated and ready for service.

The Commonwealth of Massachusetts by an Act of the legislature appropriated $50,000, which sum was paid for the hospital ship, and loaned her to the Massachusetts Volunteer Aid Association.

On August 6 the "Bay State" lay in the harbor ready for service. She was 200 ft. long, 27 ft. beam, a depth of 12 ft. 7 in. with a gross tonnage of 777, net 380 tons, painted white with a red strake. She had been well tested as to strength and endurance, having weathered without difficulty several cyclones in the West Indies when used as a fruit steamer. The expense of altering her, in addition to the original cost, was $67,000, but when finished Boston had the pleasure of sending forth the most completely equipped hospital ship the world has seen. She contained every convenience and appliance which have become necessary equipments of a well-appointed hospital. Her wards were finished with walls of galvanized iron, with white enamel paint, rubber tread flooring, and cemented gutters. The berths for the patients are frames made of one and a half inch galvanized iron pipe, on which a wire mattress was strung. These frames rest on hooks fastened to uprights made of two-inch pipe. The berths are three tiers deep and can be lifted off the hooks, so when necessary the patient can be taken on or off the ship on his own bed, used as a stretcher.

An operating room containing an X-ray machine, and one for surgical dressing was supplemented by a clinical laboratory and apothecary shop. The cold storage and freezing room, a steam laundry and ice plant capable of producing three and a half tons a day, electric fans, and a library of two hundred volumes, selected by Mr. H. F. Putnam, of the Boston Public Library, were principal features of the ship, all of which had been planned and arranged under the direct supervision of Dr. Burrell. Without restriction of any kind she was fitted out with every device and kind of supply considered necessary or desirable for the good of the well and the sick. During her three trips she gave away where needed many tons of supplies, sailors as well as soldiers being recipients of her bounty. She was commanded by Capt. Percival F. Butman, who retained the majority of the boat's old crew.

Her medical staff was composed of the following gentlemen, who volunteered their services: Surgeon Superintendent, Dr. Herbert L. Burrell; first surgeon, Dr. E. A. Crockett; second surgeon, Dr. J. T. Bottomley; first assistant surgeon, Mr. T. J. Manahan; second assistant surgeon, Mr. C. L. Spaulding; purser, Mr. W. H. Seabury. Head Nurse, Miss C. W. Cayford. Nurses: Miss Janet Anderson, Miss Muriel G. Galt, Miss Anna M. Blair, Miss Sadie Parsons, Miss Sarah Frazer. Bay Men: S. Hooker, F. P. Droese, L. L. Kemp, W. F. Lyford, Peter Sylveson, N. E. Nichols.

Her first trip was made to Cuba, where she left many needed supplies, bringing home ninety-eight men of the 9th Massachusetts and 2d U. S. V. The second trip was to Porto Rico, when she returned with one hundred men, eighty-nine of whom were 6th Massachusetts volunteers. On this trip she left Dr. J. Booth Clarkson as representative from the Volunteer Aid Association, together with Miss

Galt and Miss Parsons, who volunteered to return to the hospital in Utuado.

Her third and last trip was again to Arecibo and Ponce, when she brought home one hundred and thirty-six men. It is thus seen that the 6th Massachusetts is particularly beholden to the "Bay State" and her supporters. The account of how men were received and cared for on board is best told in Mr. Seabury's paper read before the Boston Society for Medical Improvement, which is published in full. The discipline on board was more strict than that of camp, every possible precaution as to food, sleep, air, and exercise being given the men.

The writer had the good fortune to have occasion to go on board the "Bay State" during her second trip, as she was lying off Arecibo. Immediately on boarding her the cup of hot malted milk was received, when for half an hour I sat in a steamer chair, persistently refusing to have a tag put about my neck. Having finally convinced the nurses that I was not a "candidate," and that I had been in the saddle for eleven hours, I was allowed a cup of tea and some bread and butter. This was the first tea or butter we had seen since leaving Boston. Nothing but the fear of being "tagged" by force as an unruly invalid limited my appetite. If the nurse who was that day kind to a dusty private ever sees this, will she accept his thanks?

As a medium between the citizens of Massachusetts and the regiments, guaranteeing the men of the familiarity of those at home with their experiences and needs, the importance was also great. The arrival of the " Bay State " with her load of private boxes for the men, and news direct from home, was a comfort inestimable. It was the white messenger of the people sent to the front as a guarantee of support and sympathy.

The men who were passengers aboard the " Bay State " are the most enthusiastic admirers of the surgeons and nurses, and cannot say too much of the care they received and the privileges enjoyed.

The families of the few who started but did not arrive, have the consolation of knowing that every possible attention and aid was rendered by devoted friends in a spirit of sacrifice second only to that of the man's own family.

This Commission Witnesseth: — That the Massachusetts Volunteer Aid Association hereby is recognized by the Government of the United States of America as an Aid Society within the terms of Article XIII. of the Geneva (Red Cross) Convention, during the pending war between the United States of America and the Kingdom of Spain; that said Association hereby is expressly authorized to fit out and equip at its own expense a Hospital Ship for all the purposes of such a ship during said war, said ship to be named "The Bay State,"—and that C. A. Siegfried, Medical Inspector of the United States Navy, hereby is authorized to have control of said hospital ship during her fitting out and on her final departure, and to issue his certificate as the proper naval authority under Article XIII. of the Geneva (Red Cross) Convention aforesaid, that she had been so placed under his control, and that she is then appropriated solely to the purposes of his mission.

Given under my hand at Washington this 23d day of June, in the year of Our Lord one thousand, eight hundred and ninety-eight, and in the 122d year of the Independence of the United States.

By the President.

JOHN D. LONG,
Secretary of the Navy.

WILLIAM MCKINLEY.

WAR DEPARTMENT,
WASHINGTON, July 22, 1898.

SIR:— The Hospital Ship "Bay State" has been fitted out by the Massachusetts Volunteer Aid Association, and has been commissioned by the United States Government under the International Red Cross Convention. The purpose of the ship under the direction of its surgeon superintendent, Dr. H. L. Burrell, is to aid the medical authorities of the Army and Navy of the United States in caring for the sick and wounded soldiers and sailors. You are directed to aid and assist the authorities of the "Bay State" as far as practicable.

Very respectfully,

[Signed]   R. A. ALGER,
Secretary of War.

TO THE OFFICERS COMMANDING U. S. TROOPS.

NAVY DEPARTMENT.
WASHINGTON, July 22, 1898.

SIR: — The Hospital Ship "Bay State" has been fitted out by the Massachusetts Volunteer Aid Association, and has been commissioned by the United States Government under the International Red Cross Convention. The purpose of the ship under the direction of its surgeon superintendent, Dr. H. L. Burrell, is to aid the medical authorities of the Army and Navy of the United States in caring for the sick and wounded soldiers and sailors. You are directed to aid and assist the authorities of the "Bay State" as far as practicable. When they need coal and cannot otherwise obtain it, you are authorized to supply it, if it can be spared, taking a receipt in duplicate for the amount, and cash or draft on Lee, Higginson & Company, of Boston, in payment. Very respectfully,

[Signed] JOHN D. LONG,
Secretary.

TO COMMANDING OFFICERS OF UNITED STATES SQUADRONS AND VESSELS.

[Personal.]

WASHINGTON, D. C. July 22, 1898.

DEAR DOCTOR: — Permit me to introduce Dr. H. L. Burrell, Surgeon Superintendent of the Massachusetts Aid Society Hospital Ship "Bay State." He goes in charge of the "Bay State" to care for any sick or wounded of the Army and Navy.

I hope you will extend him all the facilities in your power toward the accomplishment of his good work.

Yours very truly,

[Signed] W. K. VAN REYPEN,
Surgeon General U. S. Navy.

C. M. GRAVATT, U. S. N., *Fleet Surgeon, U. S. Flag-Ship "New York."*

The "Bay State"

WAR DEPARTMENT. SURGEON GENERAL'S OFFICE.
WASHINGTON, August 2, 1898.

GENTLEMEN: — The Hospital Ship "Bay State," having been equipped and fitted out by the Massachusetts Aid Association, is in charge of the surgeon superintendent, Dr. Herbert L. Burrell, and I have requested him to render such supplementary aid and assistance to you as may be required.

Very truly yours,
[Signed]   GEORGE M. STERNBERG,
Surgeon General, U. S. Army.

TO THE OFFICERS OF THE MEDICAL DEPARTMENT, U. S. A.

MR. PRESIDENT, AND MEMBERS OF THE BOSTON SOCIETY FOR MEDICAL IMPROVEMENT: —

You have paid me a great compliment in inviting me to appear before you this evening, to give you some idea of what my duties were as volunteer purser of the Hospital Ship "Bay State."

I did such a small amount of work on the ship in comparison to what others did, that I have found it rather difficult to make a paper containing anything of special interest. I said to Dr. Fitz that this would be an entirely new departure for me, but I felt that if I could say anything that would be of the slightest interest to you all, I ought not decline the polite invitation.

He wishes me to tell you,

> What I had to do.
> What I had to do with, and
> How I did it.

What I had to do. — Make myself generally useful to our surgeon superintendent, Dr. Burrell;

Take charge of all the finances of the ship;

Purchase all the supplies (those relating to the Hospital Department excepted).

Pay all bills, wages of crew, etc;

Receive requisitions for supplies of all kinds, from hospitals and troops, have them approved by the surgeon superintendent, see that they were delivered and receipted for;

To keep a general idea of what food supplies we had on hand, and say whether we could spare them from our stores or not;

Receive the patients on shore in tents, or on the main deck of the ship;

Give each one a number, take their names, and temperature, also their valuables. All this was recorded by me in a book at the time.

When a requisition for supplies was received (and nothing was delivered without a written requisition), it was delivered into three different lists, one for Medical Supplies, one for Clothing, and one for the Food. These were handed to the heads of departments, and they saw that the articles were issued and turned over to me. I saw them delivered and receipted for.

What I had to do with. — Everything in a Commissary's Department that I could think of or that others could suggest. I was not limited as to expenditure, nor hampered in the slightest degree.

My instructions were, obtain what you think best, and have it all of the first quality. And what pleasure it was for me to labor under such instructions!

The food supplies were stored in six of the eleven large storerooms or lockers in the lower hold, the other five being used for a part of the hospital supplies.

On the deck over these storerooms, there was a large space enclosed with an iron grating, which I called the Grocery Shop. Our daily wants were supplied from this.

Our supplies consisted of in part, that is for one trip, 10,000 lbs. Fresh Beef, 500 lbs. Mutton, 600 lbs. Poultry, 2,000 Eggs, 500 lbs. Fresh Butter, Fresh Vegetables, and Fruits in variety. All kinds of Canned Goods, Evaporated Cream.

25 to 50 loaves of bread were baked each day.

60 gals. of Ice Cream (this kept in perfect condition, and the last was distributed to the patients the day before our arrival home).

Our Ice Machine made three tons a day.

Temperature of Freezing Room about 28.

Temperature of Cold Storage about 34.

Liquors of all kinds, Mineral Waters, Ginger Ale, Pipes, Tobacco, and Cigarettes.

The supply of Fresh Beef was reduced somewhat on the second and third trips.

How I did it. — System of Receiving Patients. At Santiago we had three tents on shore (thanks to Maj. L. C. Carr, Volunteer Surgeon from Ohio, who was of the greatest assistance to us in providing the tents, and locating them for us .

The patients came to us in ambulances from the Hospital near San Juan Hill. (Some of these ambulances were upset or broke down on the way. The road was almost impassable, and as there were two tiers of stretchers in each ambulance, the patients were terribly shaken up.)

They were brought into my tent first, where Drs. Manahan or Bottomley questioned them or their officers in regard to their previous condition. If a patient was very ill, he was given an odd number which signified a lower berth on the ship, that he might be more easily attended; otherwise, he was given an even number, which called for an upper berth.

These numbers were small nickel tags on a cord, which was passed over the patient's head, and hung about his neck. This number corresponded to his berth number on the ship.

It was not customary in speaking of a patient to mention his name; he was known by his number. His temperature was taken by Miss Galt. His valuables taken, put in an envelope marked with his number. He was then given a canvas bag, the number of which corresponded to the number already given him.

This bag contained a complete outfit, consisting of a brown duck suit, underclothes, slippers, and soft hat. He was then taken, with his bag, into either one of the other tents, where he was stripped, given a sponge bath of corrosive sublimate by a Bay Man (there were two in each tent), his new outfit put on, his uniform put back into his bag (which was sterilized later on the ship), and he was sent aboard the ship in the launch.

It took us eight minutes on the average, from the time a patient entered my tent until he was off for the ship. This system of receiving the patients, so simple yet so perfect, the rapidity with which it was accomplished, astonished the army officers who witnessed it, and they complimented us highly.

At Arecibo, this work was done on the ship, as the patients were received late in the day, and it was thought best to get them on board as soon as possible.

At Ponce we took on nine patients only, and our

work was carried on in one of the rooms of the Custom House.

When the ship reached Boston, the patients were returned their valuables and canvas bags, which they took with them when they left.

And now, Mr. President, just a word or two about our surgeon superintendent. He has said so many kind things of those under him, that I cannot let this opportunity go by without expressing my opinion of our "General," as we called him. While giving due credit to all others connected with the ship for their noble work, I must say that it was to the wonderful executive ability of Dr. Herbert Burrell that the record made by the "Bay State" will serve as a standard for all relief expeditions of this kind. He went forth with the well defined purpose of doing all the good possible, as speedily and as directly as it could be accomplished.

Zeal was supplemented with brains.

W. H. SEABURY,
Volunteer Purser, Hospital Ship "Bay State."

BOSTON, Nov. 21, 1898.

The following verses were read November 22, 1898, in response to the toast of "The Ladies" on the occasion of the Tavern Club Dinner in honor of those who did service in connection with the hospital ship, "Bay State."

> You ask me to speak on behalf of the ladies
> Who shone in our bout with the cohorts of Cadiz:
> You ask me to speak on behalf of the nurses, —
> And with your permission I 'll do it in verses.

The Sixth Massachusetts

"The Ladies, God bless them! The toast never varies
From Alaska's cold snows to the sunny Canaries.
Man fills up his goblet and drains it while drinking,
But the sentiment lies in the thought which he's thinking.

Those dear little dolls with their pretty grimaces,
Their kittenish ways and their delicate faces,
Are precious to some because dainty and fearful,
Adorably helpless, and readily tearful.

The house-wives with tact, rather plump and good looking,
Nice, amiable souls with a genius for cooking,
Are popular still with the saint and the sinner, —
When the chair cries "The Ladies!" man thinks of his dinner.

The daughter of Spain with the night in her hair,
With the sloe in her eye and an indolent air,
Entrances her lover who taps at the pane:
Delicious! But where are the navies of Spain?

That new woman is fair no man needs to be told,
She has night in her hair, she has tresses of gold.
But what makes her precious for you and for me
Is the soul which is in her, — the soul which is free;

Which, bursting the fetters of fashion and caste,
Undeterred by tradition and deaf to the past,
Seeks a post in the ranks, claims the right to a place
Wherever her presence can succor the race;

Wherever there's room for sweet patience and care,
For love which complains not, and courage to bear
The stress of life's battles — albeit to tread
A hospital ship in the wake of the dead.

Miss Sadie Parsons.

Humanity calls and undaunted she stands.
There is sweat on her brow, there is blood on her hands.
Ho! dames with traditions, does this give you pain?
Take heed, and remember the navies of Spain.

"The Ladies, God bless them!" Long life to the toast!
A health to the nurses who served at their post
In a hospital ship on a hurricane sea
For the sake of our country, for you, and for me.

    [Signed]   ROBERT GRANT.

CHAPTER X

ARECIBO

THE attitude of the Spaniards towards the American soldiers who were inside their lines on business at Arecibo during the protocol was courteous to an unexpected degree and showed a spirit that our men could not have surpassed. This at a time when peace was not a certainty, and when one or two individuals were at the mercy of hundreds of soldiers; yet no offence, by word or jest, was on any occasion shown. Later, when the troops were together in the same city, a friendliness that grew into intimacy in a day began to rule. The exchange of souvenirs, including buttons, buckles, belts, and anything that was characteristic of the army, took place in the cafés over whatever the pockets of the men could afford.

During the protocol four of our men went to San Juan with the paymaster's boxes, travelling in a car filled with Spanish soldiers, landing at San Juan at ten o'clock at night as entire strangers, the only American soldiers in the city. That this was done not only without an unpleasant experience but on the other hand with courteous treatment from our fellow passengers in the train, who were urgent in their invitation to drink with them, is another confirmation of the kindly spirit pervading the ranks.

SPANISH SOLDIERS ENTERTAINING AMERICAN SOLDIERS.

Later our soldiers became the guests of the Spanish soldiers, and on more than one occasion "messed" with them in their quarters.

That this feeling was not the same for the natives was shown by the constant hostilities between them.

The natives could not understand why the Spaniards were not only undisturbed but that their property and lives were protected by the American army which had so recently been their enemy. Such were the conditions when a feud, originating in a private quarrel between a Spanish soldier and a native of Arecibo over a woman, ended in the shooting and killing in cold blood of five natives by this soldier and some comrades, who had secreted their guns at night, which they used with fatal effect against natives armed only with machetes. This happened October 9, afternoon, Sunday being, as in Spain, the principal holiday of the week, when the news spread like wild-fire throughout the town and country. Within two hours after the shooting, from every by-way and road came crowds by the hundreds, armed with the ever-present machete, flocking towards town, gesticulating and yelling, vowing death to the Spaniards and destruction to the city. What promised to be a terrible calamity of ravage and fire was averted only by the timely arrival of Company E, who, under the relaxation of rules relative to bringing supplies through the lines, were brought in on order of Lieutenant Talbot, stationed at that time in Arecibo, at the request of the British consul, to furnish a guard for the consulate. The comandante proclaimed martial law, closing every store and shop in Arecibo, and cleared the streets, but with an excitable population of thousands, hidden behind doors and blinds, all on the *qui vive* for the threatened danger and anticipated disaster. Only the arrival of Company E and the proximity of Companies H, F, K, and L, who arrived with Major Darling at the outposts the following day, prevented an outbreak as a climax to the condition

THREE OF A KIND.

of affairs that would have been a national tragedy. Company F immediately on arrival relieved the Spanish guard in Arecibo.

Meantime the preparation for the evacuation of the Spanish troops was hurried, final arrangements being made for their departure on Tuesday, October 11. During the intervening days every squad of Spanish soldiers which passed through the streets did so with loaded guns or protected by an armed guard, in this way only avoiding violence at the hands of the natives. The English consul did not venture from his house excepting under the protection of an American guard with guns loaded.

The home of Mr. David Wilson, the English consul in Porto Rico, became headquarters for our troops in Arecibo. Mr. Wilson was not only untiring in his kind offices for the Americans and an invaluable aid in his knowledge of the people and political situation on the island, but he dispensed a cordial hospitality from his home, which made the officers and privates alike regret leaving his town.

Mr. Carrion, formerly the American consul at Porto Rico, was also zealous in his kind offices of hospitality, keeping open house to the extent of making his home literally the home of Americans.

October 10. Major Darling received orders to leave Utuado for Arecibo with Companies I, H, K, and L, from which place H was to go to Manati and K to Barcelonita. The command arrived at Dr. Watlington's estate, two miles from Arecibo, at 4 P. M., where it spent the night, not occupying Arecibo until the following day.

October 11. When the hour set for the evacuation of the Spaniards arrived, a guard of American soldiers was posted, reaching from the station into the city, with instructions to see that no

ARECIBO.

Spaniard was molested on the way to the train. At three o'clock, the time agreed upon for the evacuation, the seven hundred Spanish soldiers marched from their barracks and lined up by companies on either side of the Cathedral, while our troops took a position facing the Cathedral in front of the City Hall. The formalities attendant upon the transfer of the city were in charge of Major Darling, who received from the authorities the necessary instructions and papers to enable him to assume immediately the functions of the departing comandante. The wife of this officer, with her face buried in her handkerchief, was driven quickly from the Plaza to the train past the English consulate, where a weeping good-by was said to the family of the consul.

Immediately afterwards the troops moved quickly and quietly by companies to the train, followed by the comandante, who had asked, as a special favor, that the American flag might not be raised until his face was turned towards Spain. Every precaution had been taken to grant this request, when in the middle of the ceremonies a shout arose, as a small flag fluttered up from a neighboring balcony, up side down to be sure, but nevertheless the "Stars and Stripes." Order was restored only when this was hauled down and the ceremony proceeded. As the comandante rode away, the rope of the flag staff on top the City Hall began to vibrate, when although the flag was not yet visible, the shouting began, continuing until a large new flag, caught by the breeze, was unfurled over the top cornice of the building. Cheer after cheer and storms of applause rent the air. All the pent up excitement and enthusiasm of this excitable race broke loose, when that event to which they had so long looked forward was consummated. One excitable negro on a broken-down horse with a long trailing flag heading a procession of the lower order of the populace, paraded the streets with all the excitable spirit of an anarchist mob. No outbreak, however, occurred, and shops and houses were again opened and peace was restored.

Following the troops to the station, the writer was standing behind the comandante, when a soldier who had deserted from his company but now returned to get transportation to Spain, was brought up to him. The officer looked at the man, struck him first with the back of his hand in the face, then with his fist, finally across the face with his walking stick, while the soldier stood and trembled like a kicked cur, and then crawled away to hide himself among his comrades, no indication by sign or word being made by the soldiers of the action of the comandante being an unusual or unnatural one.

The natives after the murder on Sunday finding themselves debarred from entering the city and foiled in their plan of revenge by violence to Spanish soldiers, had resorted to the subterfuge of burning the haciendas in the neighborhood of Arecibo. Sunday night fourteen were burned, the following evening twenty-one, and an equal number on Wednesday night. When we turned from the ceremonies attendant upon evacuation, from every hill-top was rising a column of smoke, telling the story of burning homes (one of which was the country residence of their priest, who has been many years in Arecibo and is much beloved by the people), as a defiant message to the departing army of their hatred and contempt for them.

The trouble between Spaniards and natives reached far back into the country, wherever there was a house or property worth molesting which belonged to their old masters. The law forbidding firearms to be kept in the possession of any citizen rendered a planter almost helpless against a crowd of natives bent on pillaging, while the national timidity characterizing this people added to their alarm. In the presence of one soldier, they became brave and talked fearlessly; but when left alone they showed the greatest terror, and would ride miles to ask for a detail for the protection of their property. If all such requests made had been granted, it would have taken as many regiments as we had men. The policy adopted was that of placing a company in the

CHARITY.

most prominent towns, where the captain became the acting mayor or alcalde, and from which point of vantage small details of men would be sent into the country.

While in these places, the officers and men received every attention from the natives, and in return the natives received uniform consideration and courteous treatment at the hands of the soldiers. The owners of many haciendas who had opened their doors to privates of the 6th as a military guard closed them behind them as warm friends. That the attitude of the 6th towards the natives had been that of a guest rather than of a conqueror was the uniform opinion held on the island.

That the natives hated the Spaniards with the intensity of the savage can hardly be wondered at when one hears the stories of oppression and persecution which have characterized the Spaniards' treatment of them for years. Stories too dreadful to put in print were told by unquestionable authority of indignities which had been endured at the hands of the Spaniards, and for which there had been no redress and no appeal.

The society known as the "Black Hand," similar to the old Ku-klux of the South, whose warning symbol was the impress of the hand in black on the door, was the terror of the island. Morning inspection took place at early dawn to see if this hand of destiny had been placed on the panel, and if it had it meant "to git."

The members of this society were in great demand, and a number of them were caught by our soldiers at different times during the summer.

With the departure of the Spanish troops, all their sick were taken from the hospital at Arecibo, leaving only a few natives as patients. It was imperative to have this for the use of our sick as they were transferred from Utuado, and as there was another building which furnished ample accommodation for the few natives it was no hardship for them. The authorities resented having to give up the hospital, not considering the order as one to be obeyed until warned, after several delays, that if the building was not vacated the following morning our men would move the patients out themselves. This final order accomplished the result desired. The chapel of the hospital, being a Roman Catholic one, was locked and sealed.

This hospital was one of the best buildings in Porto Rico, built in a square with a broad colonnade running about the inside court. To our men who had been lying for weeks in the rough coffee warehouses down in the valley, and who arrived exhausted from the long journey over almost impassable roads in army wagons, the change was like magic. To look out on one side through a row of Greek columns into a court filled with palms and flowers, and on the other down the slope to the sea, breathing the first time for months the bracing salt air which came off the sea that was the way home, was like a dream after the realities experienced.

October 13. Colonel Rice arrived in Arecibo with

MAJOR GEORGE H. PRIEST.

Company A, in command of Major Gihon, Company D having remained in Utuado with Major Priest, where Lieutenant Colonel Ames also remained in charge of the civil affairs of the district, Major Darling being assigned to like duty in Arecibo.

Immediately after the evacuation of Arecibo local politics began to work, in intriguing and plotting for the control of the city. Not until told in a peremptory manner that they could neither dictate the policy of administration, nor influence the officers, and until they had found that the "governor pro tem," was obdurate alike to persuasion and threats, did they begin to realize that a just and law-abiding people were to be their sponsors, who, fearless of threats and obdurate to bribes, would inaugurate a system of honest government for the people, before unknown to them; one just to all and administered regardless of past relationships existing between natives and Spaniards.

The native guards were timid to a degree, and under no circumstances would they appear in time of trouble alone. They moved about in twos and threes, or as many as could get together. Application was made in notes such as the following:

Will give one pair soldiers for the respect they inspire where they are.
Yours respectfully.

The fire patrol of Arecibo was gorgeous in shining brass helmets and flaming red coats, reminding one vividly of the Roman guard of a cheap theatre. Boys of not over fifteen or sixteen figured conspicuously in this capacity.

The absolute terror of the guards of the jail in Arecibo of being left alone to guard a desperate criminal who had been captured by our soldiers, was laughable. They had faith neither in the bars of the jail nor in the welded fetters by which he was held, but begged piteously for a United States guard, assuring the major that "he always got away." A wag appeared at the cell of the criminal with a pail, and when asked what he wanted, he said he had "come to bail him out."

At the end of a ride of over twenty miles from Utuado to Arecibo, the gentleman from San Juan with whom I was riding, stopped and spoke to a native standing by the roadside with a trunk. When asked if the native was in trouble he replied, "Oh, no; that is my servant bringing my trunk to the station."

The servant had walked that distance with the trunk on his head over a mountain trail, and no more was thought of it than would be of an express company here taking a trunk to the station.

October 14. Company G. commanded by Capt. Wm. Fairweather, left Arecibo at 3 P.M. for Bayamon, where formal possession was taken the following day.

October 15. Colonel Rice received a telegram saying "Sixth Massachusetts to go to the States on transport 'Mississippi' from San Juan."

Captain Barrett with Company M arrived from Utuado at 6 P.M., having come like the other companies over the mountain trail.

October 17. Four companies of the 6th U. S. V. immunes arrived in Arecibo at 6 P.M, and were located as follows: one company going to Utuado to relieve Company B, one to Lares to relieve C, one to Isabella to relieve Company E, the fourth replacing Company I at Camuy.

October 18. Four more companies arrived at Arecibo, relieving Companies A, F, L, and M of the 6th Massachusetts.

Colonel Rice, with headquarters' band and Companies A, F, L, and M left Arecibo by rail, arriving at San Juan about 4 P.M., when A and F went aboard the transport "Mississippi," L and M not getting aboard until the following morning.

October 19. Companies H, I, and K arrived in San Juan about 10.30, followed in the evening by C, D, E, and G, all going at once aboard the "Mississippi" and settling in their assigned quarters.

CHAPTER XI

PORTO RICO

PORTO RICO has until lately been in the minds of the public a far-off and inaccessible little island, but owing to its being a Spanish possession and a scene of a part of the late war, it has suddenly sprung into notoriety and received an importance and prominence out of all proportion to its size. Whether its development as an American colony will equal in results the notoriety already gained by this beautiful little island remains to be seen. The island, measuring about one hundred miles in length by about forty in width, is traversed in length and breadth by mountain ranges from which numerous streams carry the surplus water down to the sea, their course furnishing in many cases the only route through the mountains, watering the rich lowlands extending from the base of the mountains to the sea, which together with the mountain slopes make available every quality of land in a great range of temperature, affording the opportunity for the cultivation of anything that grows. The lowlands are appropriated mostly by the sugar-cane and tobacco plantations, while the slopes of the mountains are given up to the coffee and banana fields. Cocoanuts grow over all the lowlands, there being about San Juan literally cocoanut forests, each tree bearing a number of cocoanuts that seems incredible to us in the North, which are peddled about the streets of San Juan in the early morning, taking the place of soda water to the thirsty pedestrians.

The island was discovered by Columbus in 1492 on his second voyage to America, the first town being founded in 1510 by Ponce de Leon, now known as Puerto Viejo, and in 1511 the better known city of San Juan. The beauty and fertility of the island at once appealed to a population which in its occupation soon subdued and swept away the native inhabitants. A series of invasions followed one another: in 1595 one by Drake; in 1598 by the Earl of Cumberland; the Dutch attacked the Castillo Delmono in 1615; the English made an unsuccessful attempt in 1678 and in 1797. The struggle of the Porto Ricans for independence in 1820 was defeated, and the Spanish supremacy again was supreme in 1823. Slavery has been general over the island, it being abolished only in 1873.

The population is made up of a variety of people that is truly cosmopolitan so far as representation by races is concerned. Between the titled Spaniard and the blackest blacks whose parents a generation ago were brought as slaves from Africa, are found Chinese, English, French, Cubans, and Portuguese, forming a heterogeneous population the future of which no man can foresee.

If there is a court life where education and refinement are dominant factors, on the other hand there is the great majority who are ignorant and stupid.

In the very shadow of the cathedral at Arecibo takes place every Sunday afternoon a native African dance to the music of tom-toms, as wild and weird as though it were in the jungles of Africa.

With the peculiarity of all tropical countries, where the people and vegetation seem to grow in inverse ratio, the more profuse and luxuriant the vegetable life the lower the order of physical.

The ignorance of the lower classes is appalling. Some idea of their interest in religion may be gathered from the following: The district of Utuado has a population of about forty thousand. But one church, the Catholic, exists for the entire number, and only about two hundred of the forty thousand profess to have any connection with the church, and of the two hundred very few go to mass. These figures will not need verification to the regiment. Father Sherman's very signi-

The Plaza in Utuado.

ficant remark, when he preached in Utuado, that he had to brush the cobwebs from the pulpit as he entered it, is the key to the understanding the lack of instruction, and the prevailing ignorance existing among this large population, the great proportion of whom can neither read nor write.

Every town of any size has a pretentious church, but these with the exception of San Juan are, like the poorer churches of Spain and Italy, tawdry in their decorations and appointments. At San Juan, however, there are two or three quite worthy of note besides the cathedral, which latter would bear a star in Baedeker.

Father Thomas E. Sherman, who has been on the island for some months, says in his report to General Brooke: —

"The state of religion on the island is very unsatisfactory. Though in every town of any size there is found a large and handsome edifice, the services are very poorly attended. All the inhabitants of the island, with few exceptions, are nominally at least Roman Catholics. Very few of the men are more than Catholic in name. They are baptized, married, and buried by the priests; that is the extent of their Catholicism.

"There are many schools, both in town and in country. Those in the country are poorly and irregularly attended. The children are bright and quick, develop earlier than ours, and many are capable of learning to read and write much sooner than the American children. The prompt sending of teachers of the lower grades acquainted with both English and Spanish would be the best step to facilitate a change in the system of educations and to enable the rising generation to become Americanized.

"The system of burial in Porto Rico has been barbarous. In places corpses are thrown into shallow graves, sometimes without box or casket. The cemeteries are too small and frequently crowded. The state of morality can be inferred from the fact that the number of illegitimate children exceeds that of the legitimate. Concubinage is said to be common, and is not sufficiently discountenanced either legally or socially. The eradication of this great evil presents one of the most difficult problems in Porto Rico, owing to the mixture of races there."

Deaths occurred amongst the natives in numbers that are simply appalling. From three to nine funerals passing on the same road during a single morning was not unusual. Drawn by superstition rather than faith, the bodies of the dead are brought to the village cemetery in coffins made of a framework covered with black canvas, which are borrowed for the occasion, and are then replaced in the storerooms, the bodies being interred without coffins. These are carried on the shoulders of from two to four men, who with all possible speed, varying from a fast walk to a run, unattended with mourners or friends of the deceased, discharge their duty without ceremony. For children coffins made from the royal palm bark are mostly used, in form like a basket, in which the body is placed and carried on the shoulder or head of a single native to the cemetery. Such boxes are also utilized for cradles and for bringing the babies to the church for christening by those who attend to this formality. During mass one morning, I remember seeing eight babies in their bark boxes, placed on the ground in the shade of the church, lying quietly in the care of one woman, waiting for the finishing of mass for the baptismal service. At another time a box standing on the ground on the church plaza, unattended, with no person in sight, contained the corpse of a child, while the bearer had gone across the street to look for the priest. An incident which happened in Utuado, while the regiment was in camp there, was the burial of a woman, who unfortunately was too tall for the space prepared for her. The problem was solved by amputating her legs at the knees, interring her by sections.

I am sure the author of " From Greenland's Icy Mountains " must have been to Porto Rico, for never was there such exemplification of the lines of —

"Where every prospect pleases,
And only man is vile."

It is impossible to this day to think without a shiver of the island with its wonderful variety and luxuriance of beautiful foliage being the stage-setting for the native Porto Rican. No description of the poorer classes and the absolute poverty and absence of every comfort of a home can convey to the reader a correct idea of their life or your impressions as you would come suddenly through the thick foliage

A SUBURBAN RESIDENCE.

on one of the native bark-covered huts, half open, for doors there were none, with no furniture, the children naked, and their parents in rags squatting like apes in the front of the shack. An indescribable loathing of the inanity and inactivity of such a life made one long for rocky New England and an honest day's work. Men or women followed by children creep out in the morning and hunt their breakfast of bananas or fruit just as a pig will hunt its breakfast of acorns.

Gladly do we leave this existence for that of the towns, and even there life is simplicity itself compared to our manner of living. The monotony was broken by the arrival of the regiment or companies in different towns, and gladly did the natives open their houses to officers and privates. In certain cases it was from policy. In all the cities the most loyal Spanish sympathizers, usually the moneyed class, who the day before our arrival had designated us by the favorite Spanish expression as "Yankee pigs," were the first to open their houses, and were most insistent in their attention to the officers.

The native music, with its minor chord, had a savage sweetness, yet the unconsciously expressed cry of bondage, as it would sound through the night air to the accompaniment of a Spanish guitar. We were constantly surprised to find such a number of pianos in the interior of the island, and so much musical talent. Much good music was heard, but just at the time of our arrival the favorite air at Utuado among the natives, heard on all sides, was "After the ball is over."

The necessity owing to the over-stocked condition of insect life in the island rendered hangings and carpets almost a forbidden luxury, being found only in the homes of the rich, and there in great scarcity. The houses, built almost entirely of wood, without plaster, glass, or chimneys, on account of earthquakes, have the look of a boat club or camp. In the evening the doors are thrown open, and the formal array of cane-seated furniture, stiffly arranged in two rows facing each other, furnish the family a meeting place, where the soldiers were often present, conversing with signs and a very limited vocabulary of Spanish; for the better class in the towns have very correct ideas of the proprieties of life, and if the men wished to see the señoritas it must be in the presence of the señora.

The many native fruits growing wild give an existence to a large population to whom work is an unknown quantity; but that they suffer for the inactive life they lead and the food they eat is shown by the diseased condition of the children and the great number of deaths occurring daily. The better classes use more meat than would be expected in a hot climate, while salt fish is its substitute for the poor.

Of the many available fruits used by the natives bananas are the most abundant, furnishing the staple diet for the poor. These are rarely eaten raw, being cooked in many ways, from boiling to frying in oil. The Spanish wines were formerly cheap and good, and were used as in all European countries, while native rum, by its cheapness and rapidity of action, has gained a hold in the estimation of many that nothing can supplant.

The water filter stands on the piazza of every well-to-do citizen, but the water is drunk without ice, there being but two ice plants on the island, one in Ponce, the other in San Juan.

The mineral resources of the island are still an unknown quantity, although the optimistic prospector declares there exists a great wealth of gold and silver in addition to the baser metals. Coal was discovered by the merest chance of the natives using stones for building a camp-fire, when to their surprise their kettle fell to the ground, the supposed stones having disappeared entirely, eaten up by the flames.

Bull fighting has been tried, but the climate is too enervating for developing fighting stock. Fashion has tried to perpetuate this "manly art;" but, owing to the indisposition of the bulls to fight, the populace has given it up and taken solace, like the Mexicans, in cock fights, the pits for which are found in every town and licenses issued permitting the same. One of the first official acts of Major —— in Arecibo was to grant such a license.

The traveller who goes to the island must be ready to leave train or carriage at any point for the saddle, and be willing to sleep on a canvas cot in a room with any number of people. You are expected to ask for a "bed" and not for a room. These so-called beds are made of canvas stretched on a frame which closes up like a clothes-horse.

The fastidious will do well to remain at the Hotel Inglaterra in San Juan or the French Hotel in Ponce, but they will not see the true Porto Rican life.

If one objects to having chickens stray into his bedroom, or dislikes having the landlady smoke cigars while serving his dinner, or is prejudiced against the native custom of having a baby dressed only for the "all together" in the middle of the dinner table, he must not travel. On the other hand a day over the island makes one forget much of native customs, for the scenery is picturesque to the degree of appearing artificial. Topographically the island lends itself to a tropical vegetation with the best results. Volcanic eruptions have piled the mountains up to a height of five to six thousand feet, in a boldness of lines that would suggest the Alps were it not for the draping and dressing of every shade of green, hiding in shadows the uneven surfaces and giving an appearance in the distance of solid banked forests. It is the exception to find a cliff that has eluded the seed of fern or plant in its search for a home.

Where the roads have been finished, as the one

from Ponce to San Juan, they are splendid examples of European military construction, and quite the equal in engineering skill to those in the old world. The fact that there are comparatively so few miles built on the island is due to the extravagance and dilatoriness of the Spanish colonial system.

Outside the two or three principal cities the ordinary method of travel for men and women is in the saddle. The small native horses, looking like broken-down ponies, are marvels of strength and endurance. Used as pack horses they carry all merchandise into the interior, over roads that are not more than trails, through swollen streams, up and down mountain paths, living on nothing but grass, for grain as feed for horses they do not know. Yet the American officer was always glad to leave his big army horse for one of these easy-gaited, sure-footed ponies if he had a journey to make into the interior. One may go in any direction, and find his way leading over roads that are blasted out of solid rock, along the edge of precipices, or creeping snake-like about the base or side of a mountain, over stone bridges which span ravines where, hundreds of feet beneath, the water can be heard falling over the rocks in its rush to the sea in streams bordered with great clumps of bamboo, their delicate green foliage swaying as gracefully in the breeze as any ostrich feathers on my lady's bonnet. And, as if not content with the profusion of tropical greens, and the modest display of colors from flowers and shrubs, great trees blossom out into huge bouquets, until color is literally splashed on the landscape. Imagine a tree the size of a large oak, whose entire surface is one mass of brilliant red set against a background of vivid green, with a neighboring tree throwing out blossoms of yellow flowers, in form and size like those of our trumpet vine. Nature has been royal in her lavish gifts of color to the island. Bermuda, with her emerald ground dotted with the immaculate white-washed cottages, compared with Porto Rico is like a prim little Quakeress in the presence of a semi-barbaric queen of the Orient, decked in all her savage splendor. When night falls and the full moon rises over the island, turning every tint to silver, and filling the air with the perfume of a thousand flowering plants that is almost sickening in its sweetness, life is truly like a chapter from the Arabian Nights. What moonlight in Venice is to the work of man, moonlight in Porto Rico is to the work of nature.

There are many old estates surrounded by moss-grown walls, embedded in which are carved stone seats and gates with broken iron railings, through the bars of which one sees neglected gardens and basins of fountains over which water has long since ceased to flow, but which stand as a monument to "better days." The trim, well-kept garden and grounds are the rare exception. Only at San Juan, bordering a coast more beautiful than the ocean drive at Newport, are there houses half seen behind luxuriant growths of palms and cocoanuts, and through avenues of tropical foliage arching over broad hard walks, ending in a vista of blue water and rocks that give one an idea of possibilities realized.

The island has had its coterie of titled officials, who, as in all Spanish colonial life, maintained the degrees of rank and perpetrated a mimic court life with all the ardor and shallowness of the mother country.

The governor's palace at San Juan, from its spaciousness and peculiarly beautiful location at the entrance of the harbor, impresses one at first as regal. As you walk through its spacious suites and enclosed broad piazzas, seen under a light that is softened by endless shades and blinds, you feel that much might be forgiven a politician for scheming to live there. Broad piazzas, enclosed in dark blinds, furnish not only lounging corners and beautiful observatories over the harbor, but are utilized for billiard rooms and writing and reading corners. It is only when the first impression has been followed by the disappointment of a closer examination that you find stucco instead of marble, painted walls in places designed for mosaics, and cheap colored panes in windows intended for stained glass. Conceived on a scale of royal dimensions and elaborate finish, it has resulted in a huge, well-proportioned palace, finished with the economy suggestive of a seaside hotel, or our own White House, and lacking in everything but dimensions the luxuriousness of the homes of hundreds of the wealthy citizens of New York and Boston.

CHAPTER XII

HOMEWARD BOUND

"They'll turn us out at Portsmouth wharf in cold an' wet an' rain,
All wearin' Injian cotton kit, but we will not complain;
They'll kill us of pneumonia — for that's their little way —
But damn the chills and fever, men, we're goin' 'ome to-day."

WE reached San Juan the evening of the day of the raising of American flags, the ceremony having taken place in several parts of the city at one time without particular demonstration.

The following morning all men "properly dressed" were, after inspection, allowed to go on shore for the day, a privilege which they appreciated, and used to the best advantage in visiting the fortifications and interesting buildings of San Juan, and viewing the ruins caused by the bombardment of the American fleet. Company B failed to appear, not reporting until the morning of the 21st, when immediately after their arrival on board, the "Mississippi" weighed anchor and got under way at 4.30 P. M.

October 21. During our stay in the harbor, the most beautiful one in Porto Rico, we had been entertained by the preparation of the Spanish troops for leaving for home. As the transport which we had watched preparing to sail got slowly under way, the Spanish soldiers were cheered by our men while the band gave them a farewell selection. There were hundreds left, however, eagerly looking for the next transport. Continuous cheering on the wharf told us one morning they had sighted their anxiously looked-for transport, which shortly after ran into the harbor, and preparations were made for loading troops. A lighter of beeves was run out to the side of the ship and the animals were drawn on board by means of a rope looped about their horns. We were fortunate enough to sail first, but were no happier in our prospect than the defeated home-sick soldiers, who in turn cheered the 6th as we passed.

The " Mississippi " had been represented to us as a most uncomfortable transport, and it was with fear and trembling that the men first boarded her. The experience of the " Yale " was not forgotten, and nothing could compensate for another such trip. We were agreeably surprised, for while having an unfinished interior, she was provided with hammocks for every man, and the large caldrons for cooking made palatable food a possibility. The officers' quarters

San Juan, Porto Rico.

were limited to a degree of being uncomfortable, but they too were going home and did not complain. Ice water was kept on deck, and the vessel made up in steadiness what she lost in elegance of finish. The voyage was without incident, all else being secondary to the thought of home. As we came North, the gradual change of temperature became apparent, and men began to think of their blue uniforms and overcoats, although many had provided themselves with heavy underwear before leaving Porto Rico, and supplies of underclothing were issued on board during the voyage, while others put on extra suits to the third and fourth thickness. Not until the morning of our reaching Boston, however, was the weather unpleasantly cold, when the brightness and significance of the day more than made up for a low temperature. There was little sleep on board the night before we arrived, and early in the morning men were on deck scanning the horizon for Boston lights. As we sailed up the harbor, the " Mississippi " dressed with colors, we were greeted with whistles from craft of every sort and kind. After passing quarantine a tug appeared with an entire outfit for the regiment of heavy clothing and overcoats; but to have taken the time to sort and distribute these supplies to the regiment would have kept us on board another night, so it was decided to land the men at once, trusting to the exhilaration of marching to keep them warm in their kharkee uniforms. Rosettes of ribbon of the Spanish colors, held together by a Spanish infantry button, which had been presented to the men on the boat, held back the campaign hat brims from the sunburned faces of the men.

One of the pleasant features of our reception was the presence of General Mathews, the commander of the brigade of which the 6th Massachusetts is a member, who, with the following officers, were not only at the wharf to welcome the 6th, but walked throughout the parade with them: Thomas R. Matthews, brigadier general; Dr. Otis H. Marion, medical director; Maj. William H. Brigham, assistant inspector general; Capt. George M. Thompson, engineer; Capt. Charles Kenny, brigade quartermaster; Capt. Edward Glines, aid.

The Boston papers told of our home-coming as follows: —

Home again! To-day the 6th Regiment is back again in Boston; back again to the homes and the friends that were left behind at the call of duty and country six months ago; back again to receive the plaudits of citizens who lined the streets as the sun-browned young veterans marched past. It was a home-coming of which any soldier might be proud. It was a home-coming that left no bitter feelings, no thoughts of horror and fearful death. Bright and strong, with the flush of health upon their cheeks, with heads erect, and with a springing step, the men of the 6th Regiment paraded the streets of Boston,— a regiment of which Massachusetts may well be proud.

With the 6th Massachusetts Regiment on board the transport "Mississippi" was sighted off Hull at 9.30 o'clock this morning. A short time afterwards she dropped anchor off quarantine, where she was boarded by the health officials. Captain Stimpson was able to show a clean bill of health. There were only three men sick on board, and their trouble was only of the most trivial nature.

It was a bright May day, more than six months ago, when the 6th Regiment assembled in Boston, paraded the streets of the city, were reviewed by Mayor Quincy and Governor Wolcott. Perhaps, had some of the men foreseen the hardships that were before them they might have desired to turn back again for the comforts of home. To-day, after all that has passed, they would not give up one moment of the suffering, the hardships, and the privations through which they have gone. The action of a few left a stain on the name of the regiment. To wipe that out was the desire of every man and every officer in the regiment. That they succeeded is best told in the words of General Brooke, who, when the regiment was about to start for home, said to Colonel Rice, "I am sorry to have you go. I shall miss the finest regiment in Porto Rico."

Colonel Rice is proud of his men. He is proud of his officers, and every officer is proud of his company. Well they may be, for the regiment has acquitted itself with glory. The men have borne their sufferings without a murmur. They have made a name for themselves and for their State, and they love their officers. "What do we think of him?" replied a man, when asked for his opinion of Colonel Rice. "What do we think of him? Why there is n't a man in the regiment that you could get to say a word against him. They would swear by him through thick and thin." And that is what the 6th Regiment thinks of its commanding officer.

It was bitter cold on the transport this morning, and the men suffered a great deal in their light kharkee uniforms, which were the same that they have been wearing for many months down in Porto Rico, and the quick change in climate was felt by them.

Most of them were too excited to stay below, and when dinner call was sounded, shortly after eleven o'clock, some of the men did not care to take the time to go below. They gathered about the newspaper men and others who had boarded the ship, anxious for any kind of news and the sight of a Boston face.

No news had been received from Governor Wolcott, and it was decided that no move should be made until he had been heard from. Shortly before twelve o'clock the "Vigilant," with the white flag of the Commonwealth flying at her bow, was sighted up the harbor. The word was passed from mouth to mouth all over the ship, and the men left their tins of soup and hurried to the upper deck. The little "Vigilant" puffed up along the starboard side, and then and there occurred a scene that is seldom witnessed, and, once seen, will never be forgotten by those who were present. The "Vigilant" gave three long whistles as a salute from the governor of the Commonwealth to the returning Massachusetts boys. The "Mississippi" answered with three deep-toned whistles, the echo of which had scarcely died away before the terrific screech of the great siren whistle woke the echoes once more. Every available inch on the starboard side of the great transport was crowded with soldiers, — one long line of faces from stem to stern.

Suddenly some one shouted: " Three cheers for Governor Wolcott!"

The words were hardly uttered when, like the bellowing of some terrible giant, three wild, long cheers broke forth. The boys flung their hats in the air. They yelled until they could yell no more. It was grand. It was beautiful, because spontaneous. It was the first time that they had had a chance to let themselves out, and nothing could have stopped those young fellows as they poured out in these three long yells all the love of home, all the patriotism, and all the enthusiasm that had been restrained and held back in the weary months that they have been marching and fighting for their country.

On the upper deck of the "Vigilant" stood Governor Wolcott, hat in hand. Every man knew him by sight, and every man felt a personal interest just then in the governor of the Commonwealth.

Hardly had the echoes of the great cheer floated back again across the harbor when the 6th Regiment Band struck up the inspiriting strains of Sousa's "Stars and Stripes Forever." It only added to the enthusiasm of the men, and a few moments later, when the "Vigilant" had tied up outside of half a dozen tugs and Governor Wolcott stepped aboard, the cheering was renewed. There were cheers for Governor Wolcott, for Adjutant General Dalton, and the members of the governor's staff individually. Tears stood in the eyes of a few of the men who never shirked in the face of duty or knew fear as the Spanish bullets whistled about them during that memorable fight in Porto Rico. That home-coming, and the other that was accorded by the citizens of Boston when the men marched through the streets, was worth all of the hardships that they had gone through. The men of the band stood on the starboard side of the boat. Some of them were shivering with the cold. About them were wrapped blankets and nondescript articles of clothing that were seized in the confusion of the moment. The instruments were dirty and battered; some of them were sadly out of tune; but to the majority of the thousand men of the great transport it was the sweetest music they had ever heard. Its strains told them that they were "home again," with all that home means. Their departure had been hasty. Some of the men had hardly time to say good-bye; but in a few hours they knew that they would clasp to their hearts those they had left so many months ago. For them it was beautiful music, and tears trickled down many a sunburnt and furrowed face.

Among those to visit the dock, just after the troops arrived, was General Parsons, who was formerly colonel of the regiment. He was loudly cheered by the boys, and he made them a short speech, in which he said: "I'm proud of you, and the Commonwealth ought to be. You look like soldiers, and I know you are soldiers." He was given three cheers and a tiger by the whole regiment. In an interview, he said that the regiment was deserving of a great deal of praise, and he added, "All they needed was a leader, and they got him in Colonel Rice."

Not much business was done in the city between two and four o'clock this afternoon in the sections which were near the route of the 6th Regiment's parade, for apparently everybody, from bank presidents down to office boys, was on the sidewalk struggling for places in the first rows. State St. from Washington to Broad was a wriggling column of men, women, and children, fully an hour and a half before the drums of the 6th were heard in the distance. By two o'clock the sidewalks along Newspaper Row and School Street were nearly impassable. In front of City Hall the mayor's reviewing stand had been brought out, decorated with tri-colored bunting, and around this the people swarmed in numbers sufficient to defy the squad of police on duty there. Of course the greatest crowd was seen opposite the State House, where hundreds of women stood. Down either side of Beacon Street the crowd extended, all trying to get a little nearer the vantage point opposite the position of the governor.

Shortly before the orders to start were given several mounted policemen arrived on the scene, and with the handful of patrolmen did the best they could to make a passage-way through the crowds. Fully ten thousand people by this time blocked all the vicinity of the dockyard that the troops must necessarily march through to reach Congress Street. The formation was as follows:

Detachment of Police.
6th Regiment band, bugle and drum corps, forty-two men,
Sergeant Frank J. Metcalf, drum major, and
Edward Morse, band leader.
Col. Edmund Rice, Lieut. Col. Butler Ames,
and staff.
K Company, Captain Gray.
M Company, Lieutenant Smith.
E Company, Lieutenant Howland.
L Company, Lieutenant Jackson.
I Company, Captain Cook.
B Company, Captain Fellows.
D Company, Captain McDowell.

F Company, Captain Jackson.
A Company, Lieutenant Barnstead.
H Company, Captain Sweetser.
G Company, Captain Fairweather.
C Company, Captain Gregg.

Then followed a street parade over the following route: Congress, Milk, Broad, State, Washington, School, and Beacon Streets to Charles Street, where the regiment was dismissed. The command was reviewed by the mayor at City Hall, and by Governor Wolcott at the State House. After being dismissed the companies were transported to their homes. All along the line of march the men were received with the wildest demonstrations. The enthusiasm of the spectators was unbounded, and seldom has Boston given as hearty a welcome or more genuine. The regiment mustered nine hundred and twenty-five men and officers.

SUBURBAN PLACES EXCITED.

Preparations made for reception of the men of the Sixth Regiment when their coming was known.

News of the arrival in the harbor of the vessel with the men of the 6th Massachusetts Regiment aboard reached Wakefield, Stoneham, and other suburban places almost as soon as the arrival was known in this city, and local excitement was great in the towns mentioned, from both of which places so many men went away with their companies. In Wakefield the streets soon took on an unwonted look with so many of the residents out to hear the latest news, and to speculate upon the probable arrival in the town of those whose home is there.

General business was at a standstill for the time, and only the important subject of the arrival of the men

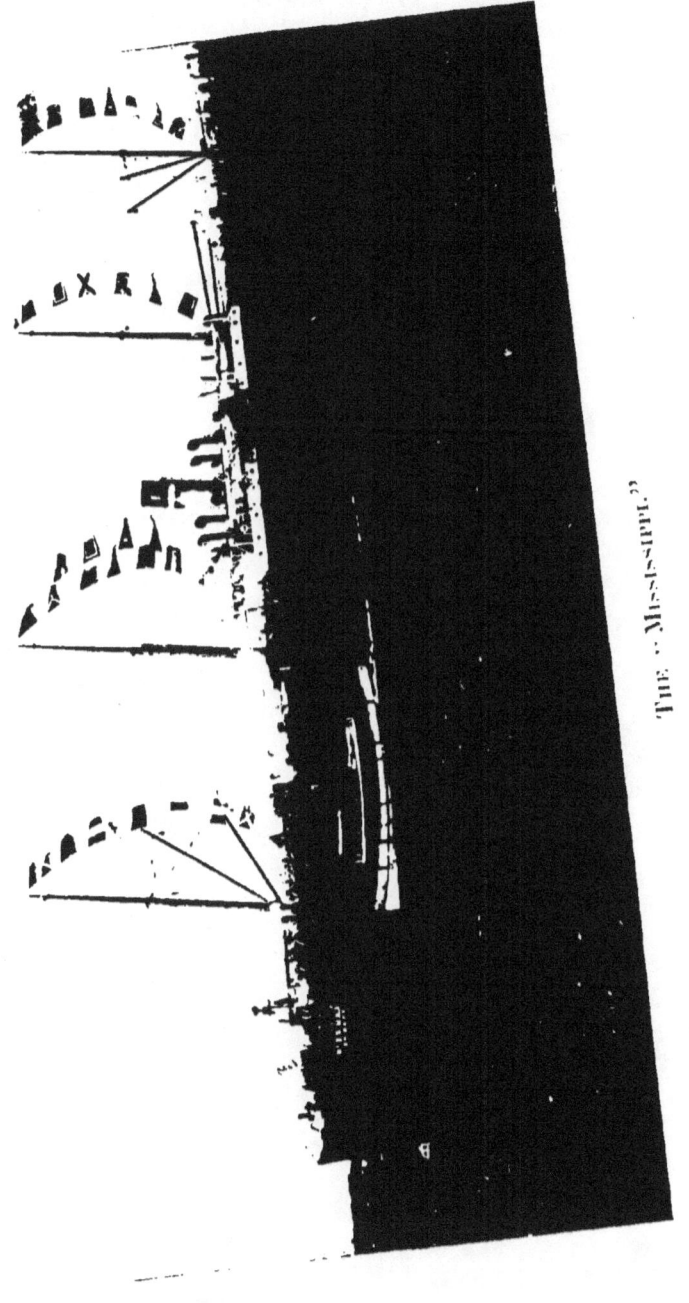

The "Mississippi."

occupied every one. Preparations had been carefully made under appointed committees, who only awaited the signal to put into operation the plans made for the coming home of the soldiers. Everybody had been interested, and no time was lost in carrying into effect the plans mapped out. A military call was sounded for the gathering of the Citizens' War Relief Committee, Post 12, G. A. R., and others who, with a band, met in Central Square and marched to the railroad station to take the train to this city to give the first welcome to the men. It was arranged for Col. James F. Mansfield to telephone to Wakefield the latest news regarding the soldiers, so that the townspeople could keep constantly in touch with what was happening here.

The arrangements in Wakefield include the general gathering of the citizens in large numbers to meet the train from Boston and to escort the soldiers to their armory upon arrival. It was thought best to provide a substantial luncheon for them, after enjoying which they could go quietly to their homes, for formal ceremonies were thought inopportune at this time when the men need rest and preferred to reach their homes and families as soon as possible. This was the prevailing sentiment, and so only along the line of march could the townspeople show their cordial welcome just at this time.

Equal excitement was created in Stoneham, which did not intend, apparently, to be outdone by her sister town, and in that place careful preparations had been made in advance to await the arrival of the men. The movement was unanimous for their welcome, and various organizations had a part in the plans. Upon hearing the news from this city the reception committee started for Boston to meet the soldiers and conduct them across the city to the Union Station as soon as they were at liberty to start for home. The Stoneham station has been the scene of a gathering which each hour made larger and larger.

When the steamer arrived in the harbor this morning the fire alarm gong struck the military call to notify the reception committee to proceed to Boston to welcome the boys as they landed. A second military call was arranged to notify the townspeople of the company's leaving the Union Station for Stoneham. This likewise would be a signal for the people to proceed to the depot in Stoneham to form a procession, including many organizations of that place.

Lowell's arrangements for the reception of her soldiers belonging to the 6th Regiment were the outcome of a plan suggested by the mayor and taken up by many citizens, so that the movement was one in which a large number of people had been actively interested. Money was subscribed to meet the expenses of giving the returned soldiers a warm welcome. As soon as it was known in Lowell that the vessel was coming to-day a messenger was sent to this city to keep the mayor of Lowell posted regarding the movements of the regiment in passing quarantine, landing, and the like. The messenger met the soldiers here and accompanied them on the train home. For their arrival there all the bands in the city offered their services free for the procession, and the High School Regiment was given permission to turn out. The arrangements included the provision of a light luncheon at the Lowell armory on arrival of the soldiers. It is an interesting fact that when the men left their homes to go to war, chime bells in the city played "The Girl I Left Behind Me," and it was thought by the committee that "When Johnny Comes

Marching Home" would be the most appropriate selection which could be chosen for the home-coming.

In Fitchburg, well-arranged plans were made for the reception of the men belonging there. As in other places, the fire alarm was made the means of keeping the people posted regarding the movements of the regiment after the arrival in the harbor here. Business had been suspended for the time being and school children enjoyed a holiday. The Fitchburg Band and the Sacred Heart Drum Corps volunteered their services as escorts, others being Post 19, G. A. R., and Camp 28. S. V., of Fitchburg, and Post 53, G. A. R., and Camp 52, S. V., of Leominster.

Milford sent a delegation to this city, and their departure from that town was the signal for considerable excitement in anticipation of the near arrival there of the men. The preparations there included escort of the soldiers by the Milford Brass Band, Post 22, G. A. R., the Sons of Veterans, and the Milford High School Cadets on arrival of the train. The citizens were also asked to join in the march. A depot of supplies had been opened for those interested to leave flannels, etc., for the soldiers.

Marlboro citizens also sent a committee to welcome in this city the men from that place, and the plans for the reception in their own home will show the soldiers that they have by no means been forgotten while away on duty. As in many other places, it was planned to give them a public banquet and reception when they were rested.

South Framingham's plans were not for a great demonstration, it being realized that the men were not likely to be in suitable condition to care for much beyond reaching their own homes as quickly as possible.

The men were met here by a committee to escort them to their town, and there the welcome was carefully planned so as not to tax their strength or take their time beyond the march to the armory with early dismissal for home. Future plans were made for their entertainment in a more elaborate way, when they could better enjoy a demonstration in their honor.

The "Boston Transcript." Oct. 29, 1899.

The 6th Regiment certainly looked well as it marched through the streets Thursday afternoon; the stain of campaigning, the look of use about equipments, the crowd and exultant faces of the soldiers, the shouts of the crowd, all went to make up an old-time war picture. It was rather a surprise to see the men looking so well; those who return from Porto Rico do not bring with them the "Santiago look." That a large regiment made up of green men should have lost so few from sickness in an active campaign in a tropical country is certainly a fine tribute to Porto Rican climate, as well as to the present commander and the medical officers of the regiment.

To take a corps that was entirely demoralized, that was sick and undisciplined and ashamed, and put into as good shape as this excellent regiment was that came home on Thursday, would be a brilliant military achievement anywhere. To do so in a foreign tropical country under severe disadvantages, is indeed a great triumph for Colonel Rice. The 6th, early discredited, has a new earned reputation through this accomplished organizer. The regiment's service has of course been nothing compared with that of the 2d, but just at this moment its greatness is unequivocal.

I have heard some wonder expressed at the Spanish rosettes on the soldiers' hats; a great many people were sure it was not proper for American soldiers to wear "the enemy's colors." A little study of heraldry would have convinced these doubters that the warrior may wear as a trophy a conquered enemy's insignia. The victorious knight has the privilege of quartering a vanquished antagonist's emblems on his own shield. The Spanish rosette fastening back the hat flaps on the 6th was not only correct in a heraldic sense, but was a great embellishment to the regiment. It took the slouch out of the campaign hat and gave the boys an appearance. It is to be hoped the 6th will stick to this rosette, and make it a distinguishing mark in future years.

The "Boston Evening Transcript" October 30th, said of our home coming:—

The 6th looked solid, serviceable, and soldierly as it marched through the streets of Boston yesterday. Officers and men appeared to be in excellent physical condition as a whole. Some faces looked worn and pale, but many more were so tanned that the Caucassians of old Middlesex could scarcely be detected at a glance from the "smoked Yankees" of Company L. The personnel of the regiment is remarkably fine. In few countries could a thousand young men be drawn together without the aid of conscription who would average as tall, well-formed, and active as the mass of the 6th. They are fully as stalwart as the English linesmen, and have a nervous force that Tommy Atkins, with all his good qualities, lacks. Such a regiment in Paris would be regarded as the advance guard of an army of giants. The march of yesterday gave evidence of a home-coming from foreign service by the parrots and game cocks perched on the shoulders of the men, and the Spanish cockades worn in their hats, souvenirs that smacked of the soil of Porto Rico. Nor was the " mascot " missing, a little white dog born in Porto Rico, who wagged a willing allegiance to the colors of the 6th. The regiment gave evidence also of the benefits a volunteer corps receives from being commanded by a "regular," who has among his associates at least two officers who have either served in the regulars or been educated at West Point.

The regiment marched out through the city, sunburned and black, causing the remark to be made constantly that the men looked well. If the public could have eliminated the tan and the exhilaration attendant on the home coming, they would have seen a crowd of men who with few exceptions were then suffering, and will for many months to come suffer, from the results of the Porto Rican campaign.

The welcome home given the 6th was a royal one, and one that made the men forget the days of hunger and weariness. Rather did they ask themselves: Are we worthy the compliment the State has paid us? The appreciation of the reception was the more intense because of the unfortunate criticism which had been made of the regiment at one time during the summer. But when the parade was over and the companies were

THE FITCHBURG BANQUET HALL.

dismissed to go to their own homes. it was with the assurance that whatever misunderstanding may have arisen or misrepresentations been made the 6th still held the confidence and respect of Massachusetts.

Youths who had left their homes as boys returned as men, having earned the respect of the older citizens of their town, while the paternal care and interest shown by the older members of society in the " enlisted men " touched a spring of sympathetic understanding and affection in the younger men that nothing else but an experience like in kind to that of '98 could have developed.

As days passed and men no longer had to " be careful what they ate," receptions were tendered each company in turn by the citizens of its town. The presence of the Colonel and Mrs. Rice was a pleasure to the men. who at Fitchburg presented Mrs. Rice with a souvenir pin of diamonds and pearls.

On Saturday, January 21, the regiment was mustered out of the United States service by Colonel Weaver, and received its final pay.

Colonel Weaver, who had also mustered the regiment in, remarked at the banquet that he " had acted, so to speak, in the capacity of wet nurse and undertaker to the regiment." By his uniform kindness and many favors shown the officers in the routine of duty Colonel Weaver has gained a respect that is more akin to affection than duty.

Companies F, E, and M were mustered out at South Framingham. Companies A, H, I, and L. in Boston, Companies B and D in Fitchburg. Companies C and G in Lowell, and Company K in Southbridge.

As a proper finish to the history of the 6th Massachusetts. U. S. V., in the Spanish-American war, on the evening of the 21st after muster out. the officers of the regiment tendered Col. Edmund Rice a reception at the University Club, Boston, where they were able to greet him in the good fellowship of man to man.

Lieut. Col. Butler Ames acted as master of ceremonies.

After the tables had been cleared. Governor Wolcott was introduced. He said: —

I have been sitting here in a thoroughly enjoyable state, and, although Colonel Ames has said that no dinner would be complete without speeches. I think that any society or regiment which can hold a meeting of this kind without speeches has achieved great distinction. I deem it a great privilege and honor to meet the officers of the 6th Regiment here to-night. I have always taken a special interest in the 6th Regiment. I will not go into details regarding the period preceding the appointment of Colonel Rice as commanding officer of the regiment. Suffice it to say that it was a period of great anxiety to me. I do not wish to refer particu-

LIEUT. COL. BUTLER AMES.

larly to the Charleston affair, although I received numerous anonymous letters and telegrams at that time.

For a long time I could get no answer to the telegrams I sent regarding the resignations in the 6th, but at length I received a definite statement, and also a strong recommendation for the appointment of Colonel Rice as the commanding officer of the regiment. It took me, perhaps, less than an hour to decide. There were many men in the State House who knew the record of Colonel Rice during the Civil War, and I therefore appointed him instantly.

The reports which I received of the regiment thereafter caused me to think that I had made no mistake in so doing. I learned that the appointment of Colonel Rice had been well received by the regiment, and that the tone of the regiment had been raised to what it should be, and it was profoundly gratifying to me.

Maj. C. K. Darling was introduced as the next and final speaker. He reviewed briefly the march of the regiment across Porto Rico, and spoke of the day when Colonel Rice first joined it. He said:

I want the colonel to believe that when he rode along the line that day, he rode straight into the hearts of every officer and man in the regiment. Colonel Rice, the officers of the 6th Regiment wish in some way to show their appreciation of your service and their affection for you.

Here is something which may remind you of this occasion, and of other occasions. It is shaped like unto the tin cup which we saw not long ago. I cannot guarantee that the handles are made from the horns of the Porto Rican bulls which used to delay us in our progress across the island; but we offer it to you with our most sincere regard and esteem, and we hope when you resign from the service in which you have served so long and so faithfully, that you will return to the Commonwealth of Massachusetts, and settle among those who will always have a friendly feeling toward you.

We wish you to believe that, wherever you may go or whatever friends you may make, you will find none that are truer or more sincere than those you see before you to-night.

While Major Darling was speaking he was filling with champagne a magnificent silver loving cup, about ten inches high, with buckhorn handles. On one side is an enamelled Spanish rosette, like those which the regiment wore as a distinguishing badge on its return from Porto Rico, and on the other is the following inscription:

Presented to Col. Edmund Rice of the 6th Massachusetts Volunteer Infantry by the officers of his regiment, who served in Porto Rico, as a tribute to his character as a soldier and a man. January 21, 1899.

Colonel Rice said: —

I am unable to express my thanks to you, gentlemen, for the souvenir which you have so kindly presented to me, but I drink to the health of the 6th Massachusetts.

The cup was passed down the table, each officer as it reached him rising in his place and drinking

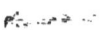

STATUE OF COLUMBUS SAN JUAN.

to the colonel. When the cup had gone the rounds, the officers rose from their seats, and gave three hearty cheers and a tiger for Colonel Rice.

Much has been written of the Porto Rican campaign in a light vein. The absence of battles, and the scarcity of reporters, there being but one with the expedition until three days after it had landed, have led the public to under-estimate the difficulties and importance of the expedition.

The island from end to end lends itself to a strategic defence, and nothing but out-manœuvring prevented conflicts which must have been as terrible as those of Cuba. It was not that the spirit of Spain would have manifested itself any less bitterly in Porto Rico than in Cuba, or that the streets of San Juan would not have been stained as indelibly with blood as those of Santiago; the difference lay in the conception and development of the campaign.

From the moment of landing our troops in the most unexpected corner of the island, the entire inception and execution of the campaign under General Miles and his assistants was brilliant. And while the signing of the protocol held in mid air the hand raised to strike, the stroke would have been fatal to Spanish rule in Porto Rico. And if that stroke had been made and victory gained at no matter what sacrifice of troops, history would have recorded the name of Miles in large letters. How much more should it do so for a victory, almost bloodless, and one more like in kind to our naval victories than anything else seen in the Spanish-American War.

That the 6th Massachusetts should have had as prominent a position as it occupied, might, owing to the unfortunate experience which called the attention of the entire country to the regiment, have resulted in a disappointment to the State of Massachusetts. Fortunately it has not so proved, for that the opinion held by those in command has been a high one is certified to by the numerous statements to that effect.

The position in which the regiment was left after the protocol was signed, was a peculiar one, in which there was an unusual opportunity for showing strength. The officers were called upon to fill positions of trust involving not only an intimate knowledge of military and civil law, but that equally difficult rôle of being acceptable to the people, while just to our vanquished enemy. Not only the majors, but almost every captain was called upon to act as " alcalde " pro tem., and hold the reins of local government.

The successful issue of all these duties was due not to the efficiency of the officers alone, but largely to the confidence inspired by the rank and file, in whom the natives had great trust.

The war has ended, and the members of the 6th, again civilians, have committed to the State their record, satisfied in the consciousness that it may be filed beside that of the 6th of '61.

Governor Wolcott said, in his annual message, of the 6th Massachusetts: —

"Under a colonel appointed by me from the regular service, to take the place of its former commander, who had resigned, the regiment won a reputation for soldierly discipline and efficiency worthy of its historic past."

Roster

FIELD AND STAFF OFFICERS.

EDMUND RICE, *Colonel;* BUTLER AMES, *Lieutenant Colonel;* CHARLES K. DARLING, *Major;* GEORGE H. PRIEST, *Major;* EDWARD J. GIHON, *Major;* STANWOOD G. SWEETSER, *First Lieutenant and Quartermaster;* GEORGE F. DOW, *Major and Surgeon;* FREDERIC A. WASHBURN, JR., *First Lieutenant and Assistant Surgeon;* HERMAN W. GROSS, *First Lieutenant and Assistant Surgeon;* CLARENCE W. COOLIDGE, *Adjutant;* Rev. GEORGE D. RICE, *Chaplain.*

NON-COMMISSIONED STAFF.

J. Victor Carey, *Sergeant Major;* Frank H. Hackett, *Quartermaster Sergeant;* Stephen E. Ryder, *Hospital Steward;* Harrie C. Hunter, *Hospital Steward;* Edwin D. Towle, *Hospital Steward;* Edwin G. Morse, *Chief Musician;* Frank J. Metcalf, *Principal Musician;* William R. Murphy, *Principal Musician.*

BAND.

George W. Chesley, Joseph W. Davis, Alfred R. Day, Arthur Drennan, E. B. Lancey, Albert C. Martin, Edward N. Mulvey, Joseph M. Nagle, Walter E. Reinhard, Frank Rigg, W. A. Simmons, Isadore Vigeant, Oliver D. Wood, Charles A. Woodcome.

COMPANY A.

EDWARD J. GIHON, *Captain*.
LOUIS D. HUNTON, *First Lieutenant*.
F. E. EDWARDS, *Second Lieutenant*.

Sergeants.

Charles Bridge, 1st sergt.	John H. McMahon.
Jas. H. Keough. Q. M. sergt.	Arthur G. Oliver.
Harvey G. Brockbank.	Alton R. Sedgley.

Corporals.

Harris E. Billings.	Elmer E. Morrison.
Wilbur I. Broad.	Charles F. Parker.
Edgar O. Dewey, Jr.	George P. Rich.
Harold E. Fales.	Haydon Richardson.
William B. Feindel.	J. Fred. Ronan.
William A. Haley.	Charles H. Tabbut.
Philip J. McCook.	

George W. Chesley, *Musician*.
William C. Jaques, *Musician*.
Dion A. Malone, *Artificer*.
John Stock, *Wagoner*.

Privates.

Alden, Harry P.	Bell, Stewart S.
Armistead, Lewis A.	Bennett, George A.
Austin, Arthur F.	Boag, Robert B.
Ayscough, George.	Bradford, Harry S.
Bancroft, John R.	Brown, Lewis W.
Barrett, William F.	Butler, Edward W.
Baxter, Augustus M	Card, George W.

MAJOR E. J. GIHON.
2D LT. F. E. EDWARDS. 1ST LT. LOUIS D. HUNTON.

Roster

Charlton, Lawrence H.
Collett, Charles J.
Connell, Henry P.
Connelly, Edward J.
Copeland, George O.
Cushing, George W.
Cushman, Allerton S.
Desmond, Daniel J.
Doten, Amos W.
Dulong, Enos.
Durward, George.
Ellis, Alfred.
Feindle, Henry A.
Flint, John.
Gogin, Ernest B.
Hackett, Frank H.
Hale, Walter L.
Haley, Jesse A.
Hall, Arthur S.
Hambly, Alfonso B.
Hanson, George J.
Hatch, George F.
Hayward, Frank M.
Hearn, William R.
Hobbs, William.
Humphrey, George S.
Kelly, Julian L.
Mayer, Albert J.
McDonald, Roderick.
McDonald, Thomas A.
McIntire, Harry B.
McLean, John.
McNamara, Frank.
Mellen, Charles E.

Milbury, Ralph E.
Miller, William J.
Mortimer, Clifford.
Mullaly, Edward C.
Myers, H. Warren.
Newell, Ernest P.
Newell, Fred W.
O'Brien, James E.
Oliver, Chester H.
Parker, Charles W.
Pearson, Harry A.
Peterson, Peter.
Power, Thomas R.
Ramsdell, Herbert A.
Ray, Franklin A.
Read, Noel C.
Reid, George W.
Richardson, Robert L.
Roberts, Richard A.
Robertson, John N.
Rooney, George A.
Sackett, Fred S.
Sweetser, Walter I.
Taylor, Brainerd.
Taylor, Edward S.
Thistle, Fred C.
Tworoger, Philip.
Tyler, Lucius A.
Wait, Nathan H.
Warren, Myris H.
Whittle, John A.
Wilson, Gordon W.
Woodworth, William L.

COMPANY B.

ALBERT R. FELLOWS, *Captain.*
JAMES C. SMITH, *First Lieutenant.*
HERBERT B. ALLEN, *Second Lieutenant.*

Sergeants.

Frank V. Gilson, 1st *sergt.*
George H. Lawrence, *Q. M. sergt.*
Alexander S. Ewen, *color sgt.*
Sumner B. Lawrence.
George A. Stevens.
George H. Trombly.

Corporals.

Albert C. Cutler.
Walter A. Derby.
Arthur M. Ferson.
Herbert N. Fisk.
George H. Lewis.
Richard C. Littlehale.
Ernest C. Meekham.
Fred S. Moore.
Albert J. Phillips.
William J. Robinson.
Marvin W. Sherwin.
Arthur L. Sunbury.

John Hamburg, *Musician.*
Scott G. Hutchinson, *Musician.*
John T. Scanlan, *Artificer.*
Clinton T. Lane, *Wagoner.*

Privates.

Akeley, Charles E.
Anderson, Charles.
Bailey, Walter A.
Balch, Fred L.
Bigelow, William C.
Bonny, Ralph W.
Benjamin F. Bourne.
Brewer, Charles H.
Briscoe, William D.
Burnett, Henry J.
Cairns, Malcolm.
Campbell, John H.
Carroll, Edward P.
Chase, Frank M.
Cook, Arthur H.
Crossman, Leon H.

Coulter, Joseph.
Coulter, John E.
Cutting, George T.
Damon, Ralph E.
Darch, Alfred J.
Downey, Jeremiah E.
Due, William E.
Dufort, Edward G.
Edwards, Clarence A.
Ferrin, Levi L.
Fillebrown, Harry E.
Fitzgerald, Percy H.
Foote, Freeman.
Foster, Charles W.
Frayer, Hugh.
French, George A.
Gilbert, Frank.
Gunn, Charles W.
Harley, Jr., Robert.
Hathaway, Charles H.
Hoffman, Harry M.
Hunt, Alvin S.
Horton, Myron O.
Jewett, William S.
Johnson, Charles L.
Johnson, Carl C.
Johnson, Walter B.
Kent, Frank W.
Kirby, Ollie F.
Kittredge, Arthur M.
Knight, Walter S.
Knox, Edward C.
Lancey, Edwin B.
Latimer, Andrew J

Lett, Stephen H.
McCornisky, Charles F.
Moffitt, John H.
Moody, Jesse A.
Newcombe, George H.
Nute, John B.
O'Brian, Richard D.
Orr, John M.
Preston, Albert A.
Reed, Harvey.
Robertson, George L.
Rossner, Louis.
Schlott, Gustav A.
Smith, Scott L.
Snow, David A.
Still, Roland L.
Syme, Robert.
Talbot, Joseph R.
Tarbell, Harry A.
Thomas, Charles A.
Tierney, William T.
Vosburg, Walter H.
Wadsworth, John W.
Washer, Ethan H.
Watson, Frank L.
Way, Allan.
Webb, Edward C.
Webber, Rollin F.
Weir, Alexander.
Wheeler, Ernest N.
Whitman, Stephen A.
Williams, George.
Young, Leon E. C.
Younglove, William K.

COMPANY C.

ALEXANDER GREIG, JR., *Captain.*
THOMAS LIVINGSTON, *First Lieutenant.*
FRED. D. COSTELLO, *Second Lieutenant.*

Sergeants.

Colby T. Kittredge, 1st *sergt.*
Walter P. Berry, Q.M. *sergt.*
Geo. C. Wenden, Q.M. *sergt.*
Arthur Ashworth.

Otto S. Hahn.
Victor J. Hosmer.
Alexander D. Mitchell.

Corporals.

Edward A. Barnes.
Herbert C. Bellamy.
J. Victor Carey.
Fred N. Charland.
Ralph W. Clogston.
Russell S. Goring.

James N. Greig.
Horatio W. Hatch.
Willard D. Pratt.
William E. Savage.
Arthur H. Tuttle.
Leslie J. Wisener.

Francis Rigg,[1] *Musician.*
Fred D. Woodbury, *Musician.*
Ezra Bowden, *Artificer.*
Bert W. Chandler, *Wagoner.*

Privates.

Abbott, Philip E.
Aldrich, Eugene L.
Archibald, Albert R.
Ashworth, Thomas.
Bagshaw, Jr., Walter H.
Baker, Ben.

Ball, Edward E.
Blanchard, Elezor.
Blennerhassett, Arthur.
Brophy, John S.
Burns, Francis.
Connell, George H.

[1] Transferred to Regimental Band Sept. 30, '98.

CAPTAIN ALEXANDER GREIG.
1st Lt. THOMAS LIVINGSTON.   2d Lt. FRED. D. COSTELLO.

Cooke, William E.
Crawford, Sewall J.
Curtin, Charles E.
Davis, Joseph W.
Davidson, William.
Delonne, Joseph.
Demaraiz, Odina.
Dexter, Robert C.
Douglas, Frank C.
Duffy, Charles J.
Duncan, Augustus E.
Dunlavey, George F.
Ellis, Thomas.
Faneuf, Charles L.
Flanagan, Edward M.
Garland, Arthur E.
Gifford, David T.
Gillingham, George D.
Goodwin, Walter E.
Halloran, John J.
Hardy, Maurice E.
Harmon, Fred E.
Hastings, Fred D.
Hutchins, Edmund F.
Kelly, Frank L.
Kelsey, John H.
Kimball, Clifton P.
Kincaid, James.
Landry, Homer J.
La Point, John J.
Larkin, John.
Maxfield, James P.
McAuley, Archibald.
McGlynn, Frank.
McKenzie, James.
McQuesten, Harry W.

Mercier, Louis.
Miller, Ross.
Morin, Ouila.
Nealley, Albert F.
Nowlan, Edwin E.
O'Brien, Frank D.
O'Hearn, Francis J.
Ostreicher, Jacob.
Parke, Frank G.
Peterson, George W.
Pihl, Carl F.
Regnier, Samuel.
Richardson, Albert E.
Royal, John J.
Ryan, Martin J.
Sanborn, William B.
Savage, Asa J.
Savage, Herbert.
Sears, Eben J.
Secord, Louis O.
Sutherland, George.
Tilton, Charles E.
Tremble, Mede.
Varnum, Algemon B.
Walch, Herman S.
Walker, Ernest L.
Walker, John B.
Walker, William.
Waugh, George.
Williamson, Dan R.
Winslow, Charles S.
Whitcher, Frank B.
Worthen, Jr., George E.
Young, Edward L.
Young, Thomas A.

COMPANY D.

JOHN F. McDOWELL, *Captain.*
ANDREW J. WELAN, *First Lieutenant.*
WILLIAM L. CONRAD, *Second Lieutenant.*

Sergeants.

Jeremiah J. McDowell, 1*st sgt.*
William H. Dolan, *Q. M. sgt.*
Lewis F. Fagan.
Michael L. Flynn.
Patrick J. Moran.
John J. O'Connor.

Corporals.

Anthony J. Conlon.
John T. Gallagher.
Thomas Godly.
Daniel G. Mahan.
Thomas F. Mulqueeny.
Mark L. O'Toole.
James F. Percival.
John J. Shea.
Edward T. Sullivan.
William J. Sweeney, Jr.
John F. Whooley.
William W. Wilde.

James F. Cooney, *Musician.*
Frank H. Noonan, *Musician.*
John J. Dunn, *Artificer.*
William A. Chute, *Wagoner.*

Privates.

Bacon, Frank L. E.
Baker, G. Frank.
Bell, William J.
Bird, Horace.
Bonner, Charles.
Bosley, George.
Campbell, Joseph.
Carleson, Herman.
Carney, James F.
Collins, Michael J.
Connors, Daniel J.
Connor, John H.
Crowley, Daniel P.
Cullen, Joseph W.
Dailey, Dennis F.
Daly, Ambrose.

Delaney, John J.
Deslaurius, Nezaire.
Donahue, Michael.
Donohue, Michael L.
Driscoll, Frank.
Fagan, George W.
Fahey, Martin T.
Faron, Michael J.
Fenton, Eugene.
Foley, William J.
Gaudreau, Edward I.
Griffin, James.
Grozeile, Emory.
Hartnett, Timothy F.
Hefferman, James J.
Higgins, Patrick.
Higgins, William J.
Hynes, James P.
Joyce, Edward.
Kelly, Cornelius R.
Kelly, Michael J.
Kelly, Thomas F.
Killelea, James.
Killelea, John.
Killelea, John F.
Kittredge, Patrick F.
King, Elroy C.
Looney, Patrick J.
Lucier, Frederick R.
Lynch, John P.
Mahan, Philip H.
Maher, John J.
Markham, George A.
May, Jr., William.
McCarron, James.

McClarty, William
McCormack, John J.
McCoy, Peter H.
McDonald, Christopher L.
McEachen, John T.
McGinn, Edward.
McMahan, Bernard J.
McNamara, Martin.
McNally, Thomas.
Mealey, George E.
Mitten, Thomas H.
Moran, James P.
Moriarity, Daniel J.
Morrill, Joseph L.
Morrilly, John H.
Mulqueeny, James L.
Murphy, Jerrimiah.
Noonan, Charles H.
Nugent, George T.
O'Brien, James B.
O'Hearn, John F.
O'Rourke, Henry F.
O'Rourke, Thomas J.
Pepper, Thomas F.
Phelan, John T.
Richard, Napoleon P.
Rummery, Charles G.
Ryan, William F.
Semard, Alphonse.
Sheehan, Daniel.
Skehan, John J.
Smith, Frederick W.
Stanton, George B.
Sullivan, Edward T.
Woodcome, Charles A.

COMPANY E.

JOHN S. MCNEILLY, *Captain*.
CLARENCE W. COOLIDGE, *First Lieutenant*.
GEORGE F. HOWLAND, *Second Lieutenant*.

Sergeants.

Herbert W. Damon, 1st sergt.
James C. Valentine, Q. M. sgt.
Frederic M. Kendall.
Robert A. McNeilly.
George O. Parker.
William E. Walters.

Corporals.

William A. Gaines.
William F. Howland.
Asa J. Margerum.
James S. O'Connell.
Albert R. Ordway.
Harry Puddefoot.
Walter F. Rossman.
Herbert W. Simpson.
George W. Sullivan.
Walter F. Taylor.
Clarence H. Warren.
Arthur R. Yates.

Herbert A. Forbush, *Musician*.
David O'Brien, *Musician*.
James M. Goldthwait, *Artificer*.
William H. Damon, *Wagoner*.

Privates.

Archdale, Charles.
Bacon, Harry E.
Barker, Fletcher.
Benson, Joseph L.
Bixby, Ernest L.
Blake, Alfred H.
Bouvier, Frank A.
Bowker, Frank H.
Bragdon, Edward L.
Brown, John W.
Bullington, Frank E.
Cain, John H.
Cameron, Donald.
Chamberlain, Walter F.
Clapp, Frederick W.
Clough, Otis F.

Roster

Cloyes, John B.
Coburn, Clarence A.
Collette, Joseph.
Connors, Patrick F.
Cullen, John E.
Dolan, James C.
Dunn, Cornelius J.
Emrich, Melvin E.
Engler, Joseph.
Fay, Herbert C.
Fisher, Charles H.
Fletcher, Warren L.
Foley, Michael H.
Forbush, Preston D.
Gallagher, Frank C.
Ganaway, Frank J.
Hanson, Peter.
Hardigan, William C.
Harding, Frank L.
Harris, Olney H.
James, Lewis C.
Johnson, Oscar E.
Keating, David F.
Kelley, William A.
Lane, George R.
Lincoln, Caleb H.
Littlefield, Charles J.
Lord, William E.
Marsh, Alfred E.
Meehan, Joseph P.
Monahan, Philip P.
McDonald, Duncan A.
McGrath, Edward F.
McElroy, Thomas H.

McMann, Charles E.
Murry, Hugh A.
Nevitt, Edgar G.
Newell, Henry D.
O'Donnell, Michael E.
Panton, John F.
Pease, Charles W. S.
Perry, Herbert E.
Perry, Louis A.
Poor, George E.
Porter, George J.
Price, Albert D.
Prophet, Joseph F.
Henry, Ralston.
Richard, Louis F.
Robinson, Alphonso A.
Rollins, Louis F.
Samolis, Thomas.
Sanderson, Frank E.
Scothorne, Wilfred H.
Seaver, George F.
Simmons, William A.
Smith, William A.
Stearns, Archer C.
Stevenson, Patrick J.
Stowe, Arthur W.
Sullivan, Sylvester F.
Tucker, Frank C.
Tuttle, Herbert C.
Videto, Charles T.
Ward, Daniel T.
Wells, Charles H.
Williston, Frank.
Woods, Walter L.

COMPANY F.

THOMAS E. JACKSON, *Captain*.
FRANKLIN G. TAYLOR, *First Lieutenant*.
FRANK E. MOORE, *Second Lieutenant*.

Sergeants.

Lucius P. Hayward, 1*st sergt.*
Harold B. Chamberlain, Q. M. *sergt.*
Chas. W. Holbrook, 2*d sergt.*
Frank L. Best.
Warren E. Hapgood.
Aaron W. Hosmer.
Walter A. Wood.

Corporals.

Frank W. Buck.
Walter A. Clisbee.
Frank E. Cutter.
John L. Grady.
James A. Harris.
George W. Higgins.
Eldon L. Holt.
Ernest A. Howe.
Harold A. Leonard.
Thomas L. McDorman.
Henry Simard.

Charles H. Small, *Musician*.
Isadore Vigeant, *Musician*.
Willis H. Page, *Artificer*.
Charles R. Craig, *Wagoner*.

Privates.

Allen, Mason S.
Angell, William J.
Barry, James W.
Berry, Clifton R.
Berry, Riley A.
Bertrand, Alma.
Bishop, David H.
Bonin, Amos.
Brodeur, Eli.
Burhoe, Herman W.
Chamberlain, Henry W.
Chartier, Frank X.
Clapp, Arthur W.
Clements, Edmund F.
Cole, John O.
Colleary, Michael E.

Roster

Colleary, John P.
Cowern, Walter H.
Cutler, George E.
Delude, Dolor O.
Duley, Wilmot F.
Estabrook, Fred W.
Estey, Frank T.
Faulkner, Arthur C.
Fay, William E.
Frazel, Jeremiah.
Goulet, Harmodias.
Gour, Wilfred.
Green, John F.
Grover, John W.
Haight, Edwin E.
Haines, Ira J.
Herrick, George B.
Hersey, Arthur B.
Howard, Ernest D.
Howe, Everett C.
Howe, Fred W.
Howe, Elton E.
Hunt, Chester W.
Hutch, Thomas G.
Hutch, James.
Johnson, Ervin F.
Keith, Lester O.
Kellette, John W.
Knight, Edmund G.
Lafay, Desithe.
Lee, Robert E.
Le Page, S. Wright.
Lheureux, Louis.
Lovely, Edward.

Marshall, Ernest D.
Martin, James J.
McCarthy, Charles F. X.
McCarthy, William F.
McGee, Timothy.
Melanson, Leander.
Miles, Albert E.
Mills, Fred H.
Mullen, Thomas F.
Newton, Carlton A.
O'Brien, Dennis W.
O'Brien, John V.
O'Clair, Joseph.
Pallardy, Fenny.
Parker, Ralph A.
Patterson, James G.
Perry, Charles H.
Pichette, Frank.
Readir, Walter H.
Redding, Walter T.
Rodgers, S. Walter.
Rowles, Clarence A.
Rowles, Henry T.
Ruggles, Harry C.
Ryan, Thomas T.
Sasseville, Louis.
Schwartz, Ardeen.
Sturff, Frank D.
Taylor, Harry A.
Trowbridge, William F.
Wadden, William S.
Ward, John A.
Willard, Harry R.
Wright, Irving C.

COMPANY G.

WILLIAM FAIRWEATHER, *Captain*.
GEORGE S. HOWARD, *First Lieutenant*.
GARDNER W. PEARSON, *Second Lieutenant*.

Sergeants.

George H. McNamara.
Frederic C. M. Silk, 1*st sergt.*
Frank A. Boyle, *Q. M. sergt.*
William T. Andrews.
Pearl T. Durrell.
Murdock McKinnon.

Corporals.

Fred W. Barris.
Richard J. Barton.
Frank Dodge.
Forrest W. Durant.
Napoleon E. Fisher.
Bernard E. French.
Wm. E. Golden.
Daniel M. Hayes.
Henry E. Hopkins.
Fred G. Hunton.
Jeremiah Leary.
William M. Prescott.

Andrew J. Cashman, *Musician*.
Daniel J. Donovan, *Musician*.
Curtin E. Bonham, *Artificer*.
Herbert C. Mason, *Wagoner*.

Privates.

Aldrich, Harvey M.
Baker, Edwin G.
Barclay, Guy R.
Boucher, Arthur.
Bourdon, Arthur A.
Brackley, Ralph A.
Brock, George H.
Bull, Jenbert W.
Busby, Samuel.
Caldwell, John A.
Carley, Bartholomew.
Chase, Walter R.
Cheney, Frederick R.
Ciordan, George A.
Clifford, Fred H.
Connelly, John J.

Roster

Conners, Thomas F.
Crawford, Joseph.
Cryan, John P.
Dane, Charles A. L.
Delmore, John A.
Demange, Levi.
Dempsey, John W.
Devine, Joseph P.
Dewel, Calvin H.
Donohoe, Dennis J.
Donohoe, James A.
Doyle, Thomas W.
Driscoll, Patrick H.
Finnegan, John.
Gair, John J.
Gannon, John H.
Garity, Thomas T.
Gibbons, Richard.
Goodwin, William J.
Greene, Frank D.
Grenier, Armenie H.
Guyette, John P.
Halpin, George W.
Harmon, George P.
Harrington, Michael H.
Hartley, George A.
Hill, John.
Howe, Francis G.
Hunt, William F.
Iby, Frank M.
Johnson, Charles C.
Keville, Peter F.
LaBounty, Harold.
Langell, William H.

Low, John.
Maguire, John J.
Maitrejean, Joseph L.
McCann, Eugene F.
McDermott, John J.
Mervin, William F.
Miles, Waldo F.
Mooney, William J.
Muldoon, Thomas F.
Munroe, Frank J.
Murphy, Joseph F.
Murray, Michael J.
Noonan, James J.
O'Brien, John W.
Pearson, James A.
Peltier, William N.
Phillips, Judson A.
Reay, Thomas.
Sansom, Joseph.
Sarvais, Napoleon.
Spaulding, Charles J.
Sullivan, Cornelius J.
Thibeault, Williams.
Turcoth, Homer L. P.
Upham, Burton L.
Wallace, Patrick H.
Waltham, Ernest.
Ward, John H.
Weeks, Forrest T.
Worthern, Walter E.
Wroe, John W.
Young, Eugene E.
Young, Harold L.

COMPANY H.

WARREN E. SWEETSER, *Captain.*
GEORGE R. BARNSTEAD, *First Lieutenant.*
HENRY A. THAYER, *Second Lieutenant.*

Sergeants.

John L. Gilson, 1*st sergt.*
Arthur N. Newhall, *Q. M. sergt.*
William D. Desmond.

Duncan M. Stewart.
George L. Tabbut.
Clarke D. Whiteman.

Corporals.

Marcus F. Ames.
Ralph H. Barnstead.
Sumner E. Barnstead.
George A. Cannell.
James S. Deacon.
Charles W. Evans.

Robert W. Lowe.
Frederick W. Miller.
William F. Poole.
Patrick J. Scanlon.
Arthur K. Tabbut.
Samuel F. Wiggin.

Frank A. Wilkins, *Musician.*
George B. Williams, *Artificer.*
Peter Quinn, *Wagoner.*

Privates.

Ames, Francis C.
Bagge, George W.
Barnes, Robert J.
Bartlett, Ernest M.
Belyea, Beverly.
Blades, James W.
Breagy, William E.
Burns, John.

Calhoun, Percy R.
Camerlin, Henry G.
Carroll, George F.
Cass, Albert H.
Cavanaugh, William F.
Childs, Melville B.
Coakley, William P.
Connolly, Michael J.

1st Lt. George R. Barnstead.

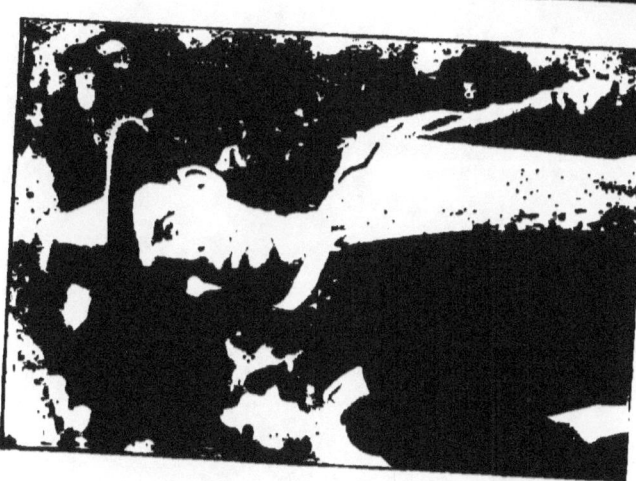

Captain Warren E. Sweetser.

2d Lt. Henry A. Thayer.

Roster

Croke, Thomas M.
Crooker, Winfield S.
Cutts, Winthrop R.
Dalton, Michael J.
Davidson, Thomas F.
Dewhurst, Dwight D.
Dillon, Joseph J.
Dinsmore, Charles F.
Douglass, George A.
Forgette, Henry L.
Forsythe, George A. B.
Granville, Elmer.
Hathaway, Joseph B.
Hawkes, George W.
Hermanson, Alfred J.
Hoey, Eugene F.
Holden, Walter A.
Houston, Arthur G.
Irving, Arthur.
Jameson, Walter.
Kallberg, Edwin.
Kelley, Frederick.
LaMountain, Walter A.
Lawrence, Warren G.
LeDuc, William H.
MacLeod, George I.
Malcomson, John A.
Marr, Edward L.
Matthews, Frank H.
McCarthy, Eugene L.
McClintock, David.
McCrillis, John W.
McDonough, Martin F.
McGann, John.
McGovern, James.
McKay, Augustus H.

McPartlen, Felix J.
Mercer, Henry.
Merrill, Rufus A.
Moore, Fred C.
Morley, Frank E.
Morrison, Herbert E.
Mugridge, William F.
Muller, William P.
Noonan, Thomas.
Nutting, John H.
Ogilvie, Walter W.
O'Niel, Denis E.
Patch, Claude E.
Patterson, Frederick C.
Payne, George R.
Peavey, Edgar M.
Rabbitt, Michael C.
Robinson, Ralph C.
Ronco, William E.
Scanlon, John W.
Shaw, Edward B.
Sicord, Armand V.
Smalley, Edward B.
Smith, William H.
Stevens, Chester H.
Turnbull, Charles H.
Turner, Harry A.
Twitchell, James H.
Walker, John J.
Warren, Leon E.
Wheelock, Frank R.
Wilkins, Fred L.
Willson, George L.
Wright, Gilbert.
Young, Edwin J.

COMPANY I.

CYRUS H. COOK, *Captain*.
JOSEPH S. HART, *First Lieutenant*.
WILLIAM N. DECKER, *Second Lieutenant*.

Sergeants.

Francis T. Jackson, 1st sergt.
John W. Hagerty, 2d sergt.
James N. Berry, Q. M. sergt.
James H. Tolman.
Theodore L. Smith.
George P. Hagerty.

Corporals.

John C. Anderson.
Charles M. Byron.
James W. Byron.
Philip A. Davis.
Charles F. Golder.
Frank A. Haines.
William H. Hill.
Ralph P. Hosmer.
Willard Hunt.
Arthur J. Leger.
Thomas F. Lyons.
Dennis A. Sheehan.
Roy S. Whitcomb.

Philip M. Emmott, *Musician*.
Charles F. Foreman, *Musician*.
George M. Lee, *Artificer*.
Edward Giblin, *Wagoner*.
William A. Lakin, *Wagoner*.

Privates.

Adams, George E.
Algeo, George B.
Algeo, Jr., John O.
Anderson, John C.
Armstrong, Arthur W.
Bent, Samuel E.
Blodgett, William H.
Brooks, Wallace M.
Burns, Edward.
Collins, William T.
Corrigan, James.
Cronin, Marcus.
Cutler, Orville I.
Dakin, Alburtus L.
Daniels, Ernest N.
Day, Alvin.
Dubrey, Joseph.
Dusseault, Clarence.

CAPTAIN CYRUS H. COOK.

Flaherty, Martin F.
Flannery, John J.
Flannery, Michael J.
Ford, Frederick H.
Forrest, George A.
Fuller, Percy W.
Gage, Charles P.
Geoffrion, Felix J.
Greenough, Hanie S.
Hagerty, James P.
Hanley, John J.
Hansen, Albin J.
Hart, Charles A.
Hart, William A.
Hayes, Joseph B.
Haynes, Josiah B.
Hennessey, William J.
Hildeburn, William L.
Ireland, Frank F.
Jones, Daniel W.
Kelleher, John J.
Kerry, Horace C.
King, Albert W.
King, George G.
Knowlton, Arthur G.
Losaw, Alexander.
Lowe, William L.
Lynch, Thomas.
Maines, Robert C.
Manion, Thomas J.
Marsden, Fred H.
Miner, Charles E.
Moller, Joseph V.

Moore, Albert E.
McInnis, Angus.
Miller, John.
Newvine, Alexander.
Nickerson, Alfred F.
Noonan, Maurice M.
Olsen, John.
Owen, Herbert W.
Parkinson, Edward T.
Penniman, Frank W.
Pike, Frank B.
Powers, James L.
Prescott, Frank N.
Richardson, Llewellen C.
Robbins, William P.
Rodan, George O.
Saunders, Harry G.
Simonds, Frank.
Sohier, Walter.
Souther, Howard B.
Thompson, Charles F.
Todd, Jr., Thomas.
Tuttle, Fred L.
Tuttle, John B.
Tuttle, Walter A.
Webber, Charles E.
White, Thomas F.
Whiting, William E.
Whitney, Charles H.
Wirn, George P.
Wood, Oliver D.
Worthley, Harry R.

COMPANY K.

FRANK E. GRAY, *Captain.*
NEWTON E. PUTNEY, *First Lieutenant.*
WILLIAM P. LA CROIX, *Second Lieutenant.*

Sergeants.

William F. Lee, 1st *sergt.*
Frank A. Herron, Q. M. *sergt.*
Harry H. Msdzker.
Robert E. Putney.

George E. Reed.
Clarence G. Shippee.
Frank M. Witherell.

Corporals.

Frank E. Bonnette.
George E. Bridgett.
James E. Clements.
Henry Gary.
William Groenendyke.
James A. Higgins.

Louis P. Hohman.
John S. Norman.
John A. Peterson.
Justus A. Plimpton.
Joseph Reno.
George H. Sayles.

Ernest Clauson, *Artificer.*
Thomas Grady, *Bugler.*

Privates.

Acton, Martin G.
Allard, Narciss.
Alton, William R.
Baker, Edwin E.
Belanger, Antoene.
Benoit, James J.
Bird, George W.
Bouthillette, Joseph.
Breen, Edward J.

Butman, Lucian G.
Caplett, John.
Carpenter, Frank E.
Chapdelaine, Albert.
Collins, Joseph F.
Condon, William J.
Coughlan, John.
Dougan, Russell C.
Drennan, Arthur.

Roster

Drummond, James.
Ducharme, Joseph.
Durand, Philip.
Egan, George E.
English, William J.
Ennis, John M.
Fisk, Frank N.
Fitzpatrick, Michael F.
Flood, Thomas M.
Ford, William F.
Galipeau, Omer.
Garceau, Napoleon.
Garvey, John F.
Gelineau, Fred N.
Gerber, Paul.
Gray, Everett T.
Hickey, Patrick.
Hopwood, Christopher.
Johanson, John.
Kenney, James.
Kennedy, James P.
Kenworthy, John T.
King, Joseph.
Kosmaler, Henry J.
Laplant, Peter.
Laprade, Henry.
Lowdon, Fred.
McGregor, Charles E.
Maher, Timothy.
Maloney, Dennis.
Maloney, James.
Mandigo, Adelbert.
Martin, Albert C.
Mason, David.

McGill, William.
McGuinness, William.
McIntosh, George J.
Mexfield, Joseph.
Mominee, Alexander.
Moran, William F.
Morrissey, Lawrence T.
Murtha, Thomas H.
Nagle, Joseph M.
Owens, John A.
Paguin, Alexander J.
Peloguin, Peter.
Peltier, Paul N.
Phaneuf, Napoleon.
Plimpton, Henry E.
Preston, Clarence L.
Reinhard, Walter E.
Rheaume, Emery.
Ryan, James T.
Schur, Fred.
Shea, William J.
Smith, Myron M.
Stanik, William P.
St. John, Alcide.
Stone, James.
Tremblay, Jr., Julius.
Tromblay, Frank.
Vinton, George H.
Vinton, George W.
Ware, Ernest L.
Welch, Martin.
Wheelock, Warren T.
Wood, Allen L.
Wood, Lindsay.

COMPANY L.

WILLIAM J. WILLIAMS, *Captain*.
WILLIAM H. JACKSON, *First Lieutenant*.
GEORGE W. BRAXTON, *Second Lieutenant*.

Sergeants.

Luther A. Dandridge, 1st *sgt*.
Frank E. Turpin, Q. M. *sgt*.
Harry H. O. Burwell.

William B. Gould.
James E. Jordan, Jr.
G. W. Watson.

Corporals.

William S. Carpenter.
William E. Carter, Jr.,
Charles F. Chandler.
George W. Floyd.
James W. B. Hawkins.
Joseph G. Holmes.

Prince A. Jones.
George W. Landers.
William W. Oxley.
Holman J. Pryor.
William H. Saunders.
Walter J. Stevens.

James H. Moore, *Musician*.
William S. Washington, *Musician*.
Samuel D. Bradley, *Artificer*.
George F. Seamon, *Wagoner*.

Privates.

Akins, Edgar D.
Allen, William B.
Andrews, Joseph C.
Ball, Charles H.
Betts, George R.
Bostic, Benjamin F.
Brannon, George P.
Brooks, Robert W.

Buckner, Louis.
Cannon, Oliver B.
Chisolm, Frank R.
Davis, Reuben J.
Day, Jeremiah B.
Dennis, George A.
Dewey, Edward G.
Duffus, Samuel L.

CAPTAIN W. J. WILLIAMS.
1ST LT. W. H. JACKSON.   2D LT. G. W. BRAXTON.

Dunbar, Lewis E.
Fletcher, Thomas S.
Franklin, George H.
Freeman, Ulysses G.
Gaskins, Alfred H.
Gorings, Jacob H.
Gordon, George H.
Gordon, Robert E.
Gray, John S.
Green, Milton.
Griffin, Reuben J.
Harding, Edward.
Harding, Thomas S.
Harrison, Lawrence O.
Hodges, Thomas P. B.
Holden, Charles S.
Irons, William H.
Jackson, Frank P.
Jackson, John W.
Jones, Charles M.
Jones, George W.
Jordan, Arthur E.
Johnson, William H.
Kelly, Bernard.
Kenswil, Ernest A.
Knox, Elijah H.
Lee, Theodore W.
Lewis, Jerome T.
Mahone, George B.
Maynard, Clarence L.
McCarty, James H.
McClenney, John L.
Moore, James A.
Monroe, Henry N.
Morandus, Joseph.
Pate, William.
Perkins, Marc A.
Phillips, James A.
Phillips, Raymond L.
Rickson, William L.
Riley, John E.
Robinson, Charles W.
Shaw, Archibald W.
Sidney, John D.
Smith, Charles A.
Smith, Charles S.
Smith, Fred. W.
Spriggs, Arthur H.
Stewart, Charles S.
Stewart, William D.
Stokes, Edward C.
Thomas, Edward E.
Thompson, James A.
Tillmon, John J.
Tolson, Harry W.
Tynes, Edward C.
Twist, James P.
Vandyke, Richard.
Washington, George.
Wheaton, Horace F.
Williams, Eugene P.
Williams, Frank J.
Williams, Oliver J.
Wilson, Fred. C.
Wilson, George L.
Wilson, William H.
Winfield, Peter J.
Woolfolk, Carroll H.

COMPANY M.

JOHN F. BARRETT, *Captain.*
FREEMAN L. SMITH, *First Lieutenant.*
ARTHUR J. DRAPER, *Second Lieutenant.*

Sergeants.

Stanley Donahue, 1st *sergt.*
George A. Wilcox, *Q.M.sergt.*
William W. Conner.
Warren S. Day.
James Furse.
A. B. Trask.

Corporals.

Frank L. Arnold.
Edwin J. Bennett.
Samuel B. Bradner.
Herbert B. Briggs.
Harry B. Chesmore.
Frederick Croto.
John E. Donnelly.
Arthur B. Edmands.
Fred Gaskill.
Willard G. Speirs.
Robert M. Trask.

Mark Bentley, *Musician.*
Alfred R. Day, *Musician.*
Benjamin S. Allen, *Artificer.*
Edward W. Howe, *Wagoner.*

Privates.

Adams, Harry L.
Arrand, William B.
Arrand, David K.
Barrows, Fred S.
Bartlett, Harry S.
Bellimeur, Charles.
Brownell, Elmer F.
Callahan, Charles P.
Carbone, Anthony J.
Cheney, Harry B.
Chesmore, Otis O.
Conway, Frank.
Cook, Richard H.
Corcoran, John T.
Corcoran, Timothy J.
Cosman, Richard A.
Cronan, Dennis P.
Crowell, Earnest.

2D LIEUT. ARTHUR J. DRAPER.

Roster

Crowley, William.
Day, Alfred R.
Doremus, John.
Dwyer, John J.
English, Martin E.
Fisher, Charles H.
Fiske, Alfred E.
Foley, Lawrence F.
French, Carl H.
French, Paul T.
Frink, Alfred B.
Gaffney, John F.
Gerstner, John F.
Gilmore, Walter A.
Gorman, David W.
Gorman, Henry P.
Greene, Harry F.
Haddican, Thomas.
Hansis, George.
Hanson, Edward.
Hogan, Michael.
Hollis, James H.
Hunter, Lloyd F.
Ingram, George W.
Johnson, Charles E.
Karle, Charles E. O.
Kelly, Patrick.
Kenny, Clarence F.
Lalley, Jr., James L.
Lynch, Edward J.
Lynch, Edward T.
Macuen, Millard J.
Mahoney, Jeremiah.
Martin, Daniel H.
Martin, John C.
Martin, John J.
Mathewson, John D.
Mayor, Fred F.
McCarter, Fred D.
McHugh, James.
McKay, James W.
McKenna, Daniel F.
McMahon, Charles.
McMahon, Dennis F.
Morrissey, James M.
Morse, Eugene C. L.
Mulvey, Edward N.
Patridge, Charles G.
Rabbit, Thomas V.
Regan, John H.
Shea, John F.
Short, Walter L.
Sidley, John H.
Slattery, James A.
Smith, Edward F.
Smith, Henry L.
Smith, Martin W.
Staples, Herbert.
Steele, Walter C.
Stratton, Eugene F.
Sullivan, John J.
Sweeney, Henry.
Wehinger, Laurence.
Wilkinson, Arthur L.
Willis, Harry E.
Wood, Charles B.
Wright, George.

There's no Place like Home.

In Memoriam

Heroes are born, not made by war,
   Or during in the fight.
The man's the hero, war's but chance
   To bring that fact to light.
Chance came to some through fell disease,
   To some in battle's strife.
Hero's the title due to all
   Who thus surrendered life.

In Memoriam

TAPS.

CHARLES F. PARKER, corporal, was born in Wakefield, Mass., July 8, 1872, his parents being Warren S. Parker and Sarah A. Loring.

He attended the schools of his native town, and graduated from the High School with high honors.

In early youth he showed a decided military tendency, and was an officer in the high school battalion.

At the age of 18 he enlisted in Company A, 6th M. V. M, and continued in the Militia until he entered the volunteer list of the same company to serve during the war. He was detailed on the " colors " until he was changed to the Regimental Post Office, where he proved a valued assistant up to the time of his sickness.

His premature death, and burial at sea, made a sad and lasting impression on his comrades.

Corporal Parker was an officer who was much respected by all his comrades-in-arms.

MYRIS H. WARREN was born in Vassalboro, Maine, June 11, 1866, and was the son of Edwin A. Warren of Vassalboro and Mary E. New of Nantucket. He graduated from the Luther V. Bell school of Somerville, Mass., after which he learned and worked at the carpenter trade.

He was a member of Company A, 6th M. V. M., nearly four years when the call came to arms, and volunteered with the original number to go forth to serve his country.

Private Warren came of a military family, his father having served with distinction in the war of the Rebellion.

His great-grandfather entered the patriot army at the beginning of the Revolution and took part in the battle of Bunker Hill. Private Warren was detailed, early in the campaign, to the Commissary Department, and performed all his laborious duties in an exemplary manner.

He was buried at Ayres Junction with full military honors.

GEORGE TYLER CUTTING, private, was born in Palmer, Mass., Aug. 7, 1874, and spent the first years of his life there, removing in 1880 with his parents to Clinton.

Three years later he made Lowell his home, where he entered the public schools, remaining until he was twelve years of age, when he returned to Clinton where he finished his studies in the public schools. After being employed for some years in the Bigelow Carpet Co. works of Clinton, he accepted a position as a finisher in the Jewett piano factory of Leominster.

Private Cutting comes of a race of warriors, his grandfather being a veteran of the Civil War, while his great-grandfather was a soldier of the war of 1812.

The funeral of Private Cutting took place at South Lancaster, attended by his company, Company B of Fitchburg, who contributed beautiful floral pieces.

With the natural love of life of youth, when sick in the hospital at Utuado he said one day. "I pray to God that I may not die;" but when the time came to meet the inevitable his last words were, "It is all right."

GEORGE C. WENDEN, sergeant, was born at Tewksbury, Mass., June 17, 1870. His military career began Feb. 8, 1888, being mustered in as a private of Company C, 6th

CHARLES F. PARKER,
Corporal, Co. A.

MYRIS H. WARREN,
Private, Co. A.

GEORGE TYLER CUTTING,
Private, Co. B.

GEORGE C. WENDEN,
Sergeant, Co. C.

Regiment M. V. M. On May 28, 1890, he was appointed a corporal. On May 6, 1891, he was made a sergeant, which position he held until 1897, when he joined the Ambulance Corps. He was immediately afterwards appointed sergeant, and went with them to South Framingham on the first call; but the services of the Ambulance Corps not being accepted by the Government, and wishing to put to some practical use the knowledge that nine years of military training had given him, he enlisted in Company C, on July 1, 1898, and was immediately made quartermaster sergeant of the same company. He performed his duties faithfully and conscientiously, and it was his excessive thoughtfulness in the interest of the men that caused the sickness which led to his death. He was taken sick soon after landing, and in hopes for his recovery was ordered home. He died while on board the Hospital Boat "Relief" August 18, 1898, and was buried the same day at sea.

HERBERT C. BELLAMY, corporal, was born at Lowell, Mass., July 16, 1876. He enlisted as a private in Company C, 6th Regiment M. V. M., August 21, 1895. When the 6th Regiment was called into service, he volunteered and was mustered into the service May 12, 1898, being appointed a corporal on the same day. Until the time of his sickness, which lasted about two weeks, he was with the Company on all its marches, taking all conditions without murmuring, and being regarded by both officers and men as one of the best non-commissioned officers in the Company. He died at Utuado, Porto Rico, on Sept. 7, 1898, and was buried the same day with full military honors just outside of the native Porto Rican burial ground at Utuado.

Among the first men to enlist when recruits were called for in Fitchburg was JOHN J. DELANEY, who had come to this country from Kilkenny County, Ireland, in 1878, at seven years of age. Always trustworthy, he filled different positions, being employed by the Hart & Shay Plumbing Co., when the war broke out. His death, which occurred Dec. 8, 1898, at the Burbank Hospital, was the first break from the ranks of Company D. The service in commemoration of his death was held in St. Bernard's Catholic Church, Fitchburg, and was conducted with all the dignity, impressiveness, and solemnity of the usage of that church. The large attendance and the elaborate floral offerings made testify to the high esteem in which Private Delany was held in the community. Father Feehan, who conducted the service, said: " I wish I might rehearse his virtues; he is our offering to our country. Thank God, he is the only one yet, but, if there are to be others, they will be ready. He was a boy of our own parish, taught in our Sunday school and our parish school, and well we recall his retiring nature, his gentle humility of character, and virtue which burned in his heart. When the call came, he accepted it. He went in the bloom of his youth to offer all he had for his country and for his country's flag. This he did that his country might live. We glory in this to-day and honor him."

Private WILLIAM A. CHUTE, Company D, died August 24, at Ponce, P. R.

Corporal CLARENCE H. WARREN, Company E, died August 26, at Brooklyn, N. Y.

WILLIAM E. WALTERS, sergeant, was born in South Framingham, November 6, 1870, and passed nearly all his life there, being educated in the Framingham schools and graduating from the High School in '89. After graduating he learned the printer's trade in the office of the " Framingham Gazette," when he accepted a position on the " Framingham Tribune." Later he removed to Plymouth, where for three years he was employed in the office of the " Old Colony Memorial." At the time of his enlistment he was with the Dennison Manufacturing Co.

HERBERT C. BELLAMY,
Corporal, Co. C.

JOHN J. DELANEY,
Private, Co. D.

WILLIAM E. WALTERS,
Sergeant, Co. E.

William Walters joined the State Militia in May, 1896, and was mustered into the U. S. service May, 1898, as sergeant of Company E, 6th Massachusetts, U. S. V. He was a faithful soldier throughout the Porto Rican campaign, not being sick until the 26th of September, when he went to the hospital in Utuado. He was taken to Arecibo and sailed from there on the "Bay State" on the 22d of October. He grew rapidly worse, and died in the storm off Cape Hatteras on the 26th of October. His body was brought to Boston and buried with military honors at Edgell Grove Cemetery, Framingham, on Sunday, October 30.

He leaves a wife and two children, one a boy of five years, the other a baby girl whom the father did not live to see.

The "South Framingham Evening News" says: "In a nutshell Sergeant Walters was a good boy, a fine soldier, and was all right."

The great number of floral tributes at his funeral testify to his worth and the high place he held in the hearts of his friends.

Edward F. McGrath was born in Natick, Mass., March 30, 1874, where he lived until he was three years of age, when his family moved to Nobscot, Mass., where he continued to live until his enlistment in the 6th Mass. U. S. V., in 1898.

At twelve years of age he entered the Framingham grammar school, where he remained until graduation, when he accepted a position as clerk. Later he was employed at the Nobscot Spring.

His genial manner and kindly actions surrounded him with hosts of friends, with whom he was always popular. June 20, 1898, he enlisted and served throughout the campaign with the 6th Regiment, returning from Porto Rico on the "Mississippi," where he was first taken ill with typhoid fever.

On arriving at Boston he was taken to the Framingham

Hospital, where he died Nov. 7, 1898, surrounded by his family.

The large number of floral offerings, and the many who attended his funeral, testify to the high esteem in which he was held.

He was buried at St. George's Cemetery, Saxonville, Mass., Nov. 10, 1898.

WILLIS H. PAGE, artificer, Company F, Marlboro, died on board the "Lampassas," August 4, and was buried at sea.

ERNEST D. MARSHALL, private, of Company F, Marlboro, died July 27th of typhoid, on board the "Lampassas," and was buried at Guanica.

JOHN O. COLE, private, Company F, Marlboro, died at his home in Marlboro, December 9, of consumption, and was buried with full military honors.

Private John Otis Cole was born in Marlboro, August 16, 1876, and was educated in the public schools of that city.

As a boy he was reserved and quiet, developing early a distinct talent for electricity, to which he devoted his time in preference to athletics, or the usual amusements of boys. To those only who knew him best was the depths of his nature revealed. At early manhood he had become a skilled electrician.

In January, 1894, he became a member of Company F, 6th Massachusetts Regiment, and received an honorable discharge in May, 1895. But when the President called for volunteers, he was among the first to respond, entering again Company F of Marlboro.

He served in the electrical department of the signal corps at Camp Alger, rejoining his company before it left for Porto Rico. The change of climate began to tell on his health during the voyage, and he was more or less confined to the hospital during the following weeks until the arrival of the "Bay State," when he returned, arriving in Massachu-

WILLIS H. PAGE,
Artificer, Co. F.

ERNEST D. MARSHALL,
Private, Co. F.

JOHN O. COLE,
Private, Co. F.

LEON E. WARREN,
Private, Co. H.

setts on the 27th of September. After spending six weeks at the Massachusetts General Hospital, he was taken home, where after alternately rallying and growing worse, he passed away on the 9th of December. As one who knew him intimately said: "In his death Marlboro sustained the loss of one of her noblest sons," and of him it might also be said. "Were all for whom he did a kind act to bring a blossom to his grave, there would be no dearth of flowers to mark the spot where sleeps an honored citizen and a true soldier."

Louis Sasseville, private of Company F, Marlboro, died at his home, Marlboro, December 30, of heart disease; buried with full military honors, January 2, 1899.

Leon E. Warren, private, son of Alby J. and Elvira L. Warren, was born in Stowe, Mass., March 13, 1879.

When quite young his parents moved to Winchester, Mass., where he began his education in the public schools of that town. At the age of sixteen he finished his education at a private school in Stoneham, and went to work for Copeland & Bowser, Stoneham; leaving that firm to enter the employ of the McKay Machine Co. of Winchester. He worked about a year for these two firms, at different times assisting his father at the mason's trade. After severing his connections with the McKay Machine Co., he started to learn the plumber's trade, but had not completed his apprenticeship when his company was called to arms.

Previous to his enlistment in the U. S. service he had been a member of Company H, 6th Massachusetts, for about a year and five months.

He was an enthusiastic member, and when the call came he enlisted with his company, as his father did in the Civil War.

He proved to be a faithful and obedient soldier, doing whatever duty was assigned to him cheerfully and well; always ready to assist a comrade in every way possible

He probably contracted typhoid fever at Falls Church, Va., near Camp Alger, where his company did ten days' provost duty. He was sent to the First Division Hospital, June 21, and was transferred to the U. S. General Hospital at Fort Myer, June 25. His condition was such that in spite of the excellent care he received, his life could not be saved, and he died the following day, Sunday, June 26, at 5 P.M.

Leon E. Warren was the first man of the 6th Massachusetts Volunteers to give up his life in the Spanish-American War, and he gave it as nobly and just as freely as did those members of the old 6th in the war of '61.

RALPH PRESCOTT HOSMER, corporal, of Company I, 6th Massachusetts, U. S. V., was born in Concord, Massachusetts, May 25, 1877, and died in Utuado, Porto Rico, September 11, 1898. That Ralph Hosmer was found amongst the first volunteers in the Spanish-American War surprised no one who knew his ancestry, — a boy whose great-great-grandfather was Joseph Hosmer, Adjutant of Colonel Barrett's regiment of Minute Men and a participant in the Concord fight of April 19, 1875; whose father was a veteran of the Civil War, a member of the company of volunteers which left Concord April 19, 1861, who was taken prisoner at the first battle of Bull Run, dying eventually of sickness contracted in Libby Prison.

Previous to the breaking out of the war, he had served in Company I, 6th Regiment United States militia, about three and a half years, during the two latter of which he was a corporal. He was the second of three sons of Cyrus and Anna E. Hosmer. He was employed at the Old Colony Trust Company of Boston when he enlisted, and was senior corporal in Company I.

GEORGE EDWARD ADAMS, private, Company I, 6th Massachusetts U. S. V., born in Providence, R. I., April 13, 1878, died in Utuado, Porto Rico, Oct. 10, 1898.

RALPH PRESCOTT HOSMER,
Corporal, Co. I.

GEORGE EDWARD ADAMS,
Private, Co. I.

CHARLES ABRAHAM HART,
Private, Co. I.

GEORGE HENRY SAYLES,
Corporal, Co. K.

Private Adams was a resident of Waltham, Mass., being employed as a hotel clerk in the city of Boston until the time of his enlistment in Capt. Cyrus H. Cook's Company I, 6th Massachusetts Regiment of U. S. Volunteers. He was mustered into the United States service on June 17, 1898, at Concord, Mass., by Capt. Cyrus H. Cook, and joined the company at Camp Russell A. Alger, Falls Church, Virginia, on June 27, 1898. Private Adams was the only son of Frank Adams of Waltham, Mass., having done no previous military service.

Private Adams was detailed as special hospital nurse in Utuado, Porto Rico, where he did faithful and efficient service. He here contracted typhoid fever, which terminated fatally after an illness of one month.

CHARLES ABRAHAM HART, son of Charles S. Hart, Deputy Superintendent of the Massachusetts Reformatory at Concord, was born in Springfield, Mass., Sept. 30, 1881, and enlisted in Company I, 6th Massachusetts Infantry, on Bunker Hill Day, June 17, 1898. A member of the Concord High School at the time of his enlistment, and only sixteen years of age. Joining the company with his elder brother, William A. Hart, who was eighteen, he went with his regiment to foreign service.

Upon arrival at Porto Rico "Carl" entered the hospital service to care for his brother, who had been stricken with typhoid fever. His brother's return to this country on a hospital ship left the young lad alone in that distant land. He was separated for weeks from his regiment, working hard and faithfully in the hospital among the sick; a favorite with Major Dow and Lieutenant Gross, with whom he worked, because of his unswerving attention to duty.

But hardships on the "Yale," weary hours with the sick, long marches, and climatic conditions at last told on the superb young body, and thus when he was finally attacked with the dread typhoid he fell an easy victim. He passed away on the 26th of September, four days before his seventeenth birthday. His body was brought home with his regiment on the transport "Mississippi," and buried with military honors in the far-famed and beautiful Sleepy Hollow Cemetery in Old Concord.

He was a lover of nature, and pre-eminent in all manly sports, a member of the Union Church at Concord, and president of the Young People's Society of Christian Endeavor connected with his church. He died beloved and deeply mourned by all with whom he was associated.

GEORGE HENRY SAYLES, corporal. To the unnumbered heroes who have freely and joyously given life for their native land, their country owes a debt greater than can be measured in words or can ever be known. Such a hero was George Henry Sayles, born in Southbridge July 2, 1876. He attended the public schools, and Dudley Academy; while a child, was always playing soldier. When seventeen he joined the Southbridge militia, unknown to his parents. His father took him out, but he said that when he was twenty-one he would join again. This purpose he carried out, was soon promoted to corporal, and was the first one to sign his name to enlist, when the war with Spain broke out.

He went to Porto Rico with the company, and was in the battle of Guanica. His friend and constant companion, Sergeant C. G. Shippee, who was near him in the fight, says of him " he was a fearless soldier, never excited, but always acting with promptness, and as a corporal set an example that any soldier should be proud to follow." Though not wounded by bullets, he was injured by cactus thorns, due to his pressing down the bushes in front of his men, doing it to save them from the poisonous spikes. This necessitated his going to the hospital for a short time. About September 1, he was taken with typhoid fever, from which he died at Fortress Monroe, Virginia, Oct. 28, 1898.

MARTIN WELCH,
Private, Co. K.

CHARLES EDWARD MCGREGOR,
Private, Co. K.

JOHN E. RILEY,
Private, Co. L.

PATRICK KELLY,
Private, Co. M.

His letters home were always full of the warmest affection to his mother and all the rest at home, of trust in God, and devotion to duty, never a word of complaint. The last words written home (October 18) were: "Love to all, and a big share for yourself and pa. God bless us all." He was promoted to sergeant, but owing to his sickness was unable to act as such.

MARTIN WELCH, private. He was born in Southbridge, Mass., in 1865, and was a son of Mr. and Mrs. Thomas Welch, who are among the oldest inhabitants of the town.

After graduating from the public school, he was employed in the Hamilton Print Works, afterwards in the American Optical Glass Works, until he enlisted. Although not a member of the local company, never having taken any interest in the militia, he, like many other patriotic young men, recognized his country's call, and responded courageously. He was stricken before leaving Camp Alger for Porto Rico, and the fatal fever quickly brought his life to a close.

He was buried in Arlington Cemetery, Washington, D. C., and through some unfortunate mistake no notice of his death was received by his parents, and nothing was known of it until a month after his burial, when they learned the sad fact, and had his remains brought home and buried in the family plot, with military honors, Aug. 24, 1898.

CHARLES EDWARD MCGREGOR was born in Eastport, Maine, Nov. 13, 1867, and came to Marlboro, Mass., in June, 1888, where he was married in July, 1892.

He had formerly been a member of Company F, 6th Regiment, but when the war broke out he was living at Faneuil, working at his trade as a gas-fitter, when he enlisted May 6, at Southbridge, as a member of Company K, of Southbridge. After reaching Camp Alger he was transferred to the hospital corps.

When the regiment left for Porto Rico, he accompanied it, taking part in the battle of Guanica, and marching with the regiment to Ponce.

Later malarial fever attacked him, and he was in the hospital for nearly a month, when he was sent home on the hospital ship "Bay State," reaching Boston September 27. He was transferred to the Massachusetts General Hospital, where he was furloughed the same day, and taken to his father's home (Charles W. McGregor), at Marlboro.

Typhoid soon developed, and on October 6 he was taken to the hospital in South Framingham, where he died Sunday evening, October 9, aged 30 years, 11 months, and 26 days, leaving a widow and two children. Charles McGregor was a member of the Immanuel Baptist Church of Newton. The interment was at Eastport, Maine.

JOHN E. RILEY, the only member lost from Company L, was born on Endicott Street, North End, in 1862, being 37 years of age, a son of the first colored coachman ever in Boston. His father died when he was but three years old, his mother when he was but seventeen years of age. Before enlisting he was employed by A. Shuman, although he had passed the examination for fireman of the Boston fire department, but was at that time disqualified on account of his color.

He was educated at the Phillips Grammar School, and was an honored member of the Knight of the World Lodge of Good Templars.

He was amongst the first volunteers in Company L, when the call for recruits was sounded.

He was married about twelve years ago to Miss Eliza Beatrice McClellan, who survives him.

PATRICK KELLY was born in Tyrone, Ireland, on St. Patrick's Day, 1865, and began his martial life at the age of fifteen by entering the English army, where he served eight years, six of which were spent in India. He was

PAUL T. FRENCH,
Private, Co. M.

ASA B. TRASK,
Sergeant, Co. M.

ARTHUR L. WILKINSON,
Private, Co. M.

CHARLES E. JOHNSON,
Private, Co. M.

discharged in 1888 at his own request, in order to sail for this country with his young wife. In 1895, he settled in Milford, and was employed in the machine shops in Oakdale, joining Company M, 6th Regiment, in 1896, of which he was a member until the time of his death, volunteering his services with the company in the Spanish-American War. He returned with the regiment on the "Mississippi" from Porto Rico, reaching Milford, October 26, apparently well. Only a few days after, however, he was taken suddenly ill with typhoid, and after a short illness died at his home, November 27. He was buried with martial honors in Milford, Mass., Nov. 30, 1898.

On November 6 a memorial service was held at Oakdale, Mass., for Private PAUL T. FRENCH, of Company M, 6th Massachusetts, U. S. V., attended by his company. Paul French enlisted in the company April 5, '98, and joined it at Camp Alger the 17th of June, a volunteer in the United States service. Going to Porto Rico with the regiment, he took part in the only battle fought by the regiment at Guanica, afterwards being detailed as guard at General Garretson's headquarters, where he remained until August 19.

On October 11, he was reported sick, being transferred to the hospital ship "Bay State" on the 19th, but was not considered seriously ill. He failed rapidly and died October 24, thirty-six hours out of port, and was buried at sea.

In a letter written during the summer to his mother, he said: "He who watches over us in times of peace will watch over us in time of war, and we will leave it all to Him who knows best. Hold up your heads and be proud of us, for we will be true soldiers."

ASA B. TRASK, sergeant, was born in Yarmouth, N. S., Oct. 24, 1876, and came to Milford in 1887. He began his military career by joining Company M, December 7, 1894, and was mustered into the State service April 5, 1895. He received his first promotion on Nov. 9, 1897, when he was made a corporal, in which capacity he served until May 6, 1898, when he was appointed sergeant and was mustered into the United States service in that grade May 13. While in Camp Alger, Va., he several times took command of the company while at drill. He shared in all the marches, and was usually right guide of Company M. At Adjuntas, after a long, hard march over the highest mountain road in Porto Rico, he seemed completely tired out and complained of a bad headache, and the following afternoon was sent to the 6th Massachusetts Hospital, where he grew steadily worse each day until his death, Aug. 23, 1898. He was buried at Adjuntas by the Hospital Corps, his regiment being then at Utuado.

ARTHUR L. WILKINSON was born in Winchendon, Mass., June 19, 1877. In 1885, he removed to Springfield. He was employed early in life as a bell boy, and worked in a cycle shop, later driving the stage at Spofford Springs.

In June, 1898, he went to Milford, Mass., to visit his grandfather, A. L. Wilkinson, when he decided to join Company M of that city, having a brother already in the United States Navy. He joined Company M, 6th Massachusetts, U. S. V., at Camp Alger, Va., June 21, 1898, and accompanied the regiment on the "Yale" off Santiago, and went to Guanica, Porto Rico, and was with the company on the Yauco road. On the marches he was unusually strong, and nothing appeared to bother him. August 13 he was taken sick at Adjuntas and on the 17th was ordered to quarters on account of muscular rheumatism, and August 20 was sent to the division hospital at Utuado, where he died of rheumatic fever on Sept. 1, 1898. He was buried in the rear of the native cemetery at Utuado, September 3, with military honors.

Private CHARLES E. JOHNSON, Company M, died Jan. 20, 1899, at Milford, Mass.

www.ingramcontent.com/pod-product-compliance
Lightning Source LLC
Chambersburg PA
CBHW030405230426
43664CB00007BB/762